BEYOND THE VEIL

A Journey into Intimacy with God

ALFRED TAGOE

BEYOND THE VEIL

Alfred Tagoe
ISBN: 9781720908890
Copyright © 2021 by Alfred Tagoe Ministries

Printed in the United States of America
Unless otherwise noted, all Scripture is taken from The New King James Version copyright © 1982 Thomas Nelson, Inc. Used by permission. All rights reserved.

*Scripture text in bold or italics is the emphasis of the author.

DEDICATION

I wish to dedicate this book to my lovely wife, Angelina, for being my friend and partner in this life and ministry. Honey, you are the wind underneath my sails. Also, to my three children Jezaniah, Jaeda, and Joshua for always reminding me to strive to be the best I can be. Let us continue to grow in intimacy with God and each other. I love you!

ACKNOWLEDGEMENTS

I want to first give thanks to my Father in Heaven for His gracious invitation to have an intimate relationship with Him through Jesus Christ. Thanks to the Holy Ghost, my friend, and Senior Partner, for His insight and companionship. Without Him, intimacy with the Godhead would be impossible!

To my wife, life partner, and co-pastor I want to say, **thank you** for your unwavering support and encouragement along this journey of faith we have been on for almost twenty years, and counting. After God, you and our children have been my rock both in life and ministry. I believe the best is yet to come for us!

Thanks to my Oasis of Love Community Church family for your care and support of my leadership and ministry. If I have been able to see and reach far, it is because I had strong shoulders to stand on. Let us continue to press on together to encounter Him, equip people, and change our world.

Finally, I am grateful to Shanda Harris and Ramona Whitehurst for their editing and proof-reading; Miracle for retrieving the manuscript when it became corrupted; and everyone who helped in any way to make this project a success. I thank you for your sacrifice and labor of love. May the grace and peace of God be multiplied unto you as you grow in intimacy with Him. God bless you!

CONTENTS

FOREWORD

Recently at a meeting of Apostolic leaders in Columbus, Ohio I asked Alfred to do a devotional on the perplexing question of why the disciples following the Resurrection of Jesus could not recognize Him immediately. After all, they had spent three years with Him in every conceivable life situation. They had watched Him die on a cross while the spectacle was viewed by the general public. Finally, they knew where He was buried; in the tomb owned by a well-known figure in Jerusalem. One would think His disciples would be the first to proclaim the Resurrection event. However, most of them did not. Why?

One of the reasons was because they were looking to His form rather than His voice. Jesus said in John 10:27, *"My sheep hear my voice..."* We must remember that the Resurrection was a tremendous transition period not only for His followers, but for the history of the world. He did not appear to them and He will not appear to us like He did in the last transition. They got stuck on His form: e.g., the walk to Emmaus; on the bank of the Sea of Galilee; and at the tomb on Easter morning. But those who recognized His voice at the end of the day (Mary and John) knew immediately it was Him. Why? The answer is they pursued spiritual intimacy with His Spirit during the days of His earthly ministry. One of the lessons here is intimacy before ministry.

Intimacy is therefore where Brother Tagoe takes us in this well written book, *"Beyond the Veil"*. Among other images and analogies herein, Alfred takes us on a sacred journey through Scripture by looking at the type and shadow of the Old Testament Tabernacle of Moses. This movable structure contained three principal areas: The Outer Court, The Inner Court, and The Most Holy place (Holy of Holies). With amazing connectivity, Alfred is our tour guide for the expanded meaning these three areas of this Old Testament icon and at every point he relates it to our spiritual journey with Jesus. Herein, the journey becomes the destination and intimacy with our Lord is the result.

You will not read this book only once. You will read and re-read as God puts in your Spirit the draw and the hunger to "know Him and to make Him known." I highly recommend this read to the Body of Christ and I look forward to my own copy. There are many books on the market today about devotion and intimacy with Christ. I predict this one will be at the top of your list for a long time to come. Read, Mark, Learn, and inwardly Digest.

Dr. Scott T. Kelso
Author *Biblical Eldership: Back to the Future with Spirit Filled Leadership in the Local Church*. General Overseer, 5 Points-Greater Columbus Apostolic Network, Columbus, Ohio

ENDORSEMENTS

Reading *"Behind the Veil"* has further enriched my understanding of intimacy with God and ignited a new and stronger desire in me to get closer to my Father. This is excellent reading material for every good Christian.

Rev. Ekow Eshun
Senior Pastor, Revival Life Outreach Church, Ghana.

Alfred Tagoe's book *"Beyond the Veil"* is an end of the age revelation that will release a 2020 vision to the global body of Christ. This revelation will take her into her greatest and final expression as a House of Prayer, preparing the earth for the tangible presence of God and the coming of His Son back to the planet. Before the Lord returns Christs' church is going to go from outer court praying of past generations for temporal requests, to Holy of Holies prayers of the last generation for the eternal request of His praying church for the very presence of His literal return into the earth.

Alfred Tagoe is truly a man of prayer with a love for God's presence and for His appearing, with a mandate on his life to teach a generation How to Pray to enter the very presence of the Lord. I have had the privilege of spending many hours with Alfred Tagoe in prayer over our years together. From the first time I met him in a prayer meeting over 15 years ago, to the transformation of the Urban centers of our city through all-night prayer meetings, as my associate minister of prayer in our City-Wide Outreach Church that witnessed over 10,000 souls come to Christ from 2003-2008, Alfred Tagoe has had a unique anointing to usher a generation into the presence of the Lord through *"Behind the Veil"* praying.

I highly recommend the reading of this book, *"Beyond the Veil"*.

Brondon Mathis
Director, Yeshua Life House of Prayer & Hope for Columbus

If there is anything God requires from his creation, especially mankind, it is relationship. The ultimate purpose for creation was for God to have a relationship with us which was born out of love. It takes genuine love to give the recipient part of you and your existence. God shared Himself with us, mankind: *"So God created man in His own image; in the image of God He created him; male and female He created them"* **Gen.1:27**. Although man lost it to Satan, again, we see God extending the never-ending love to us through His son, Jesus Christ: *"For God so loved the world that He gave His only begotten Son, that whoever believes in Him should not perish but have everlasting life"* **John 3:16**. It is obvious that mankind never knew how to love God in return. The problem is still pertinent today, we still don't know how to respond to God's love or approach Him. Relationship can be learnt. I believe this is what this masterpiece will help its readers to comprehend. The author takes his reader beyond the veil, beyond the surface, beyond the facade to the nitty gritty of what our relationship with God should look like. This will enhance our personal walk with Him which will ultimately metamorphose to our work for Him. Christianity, church service becomes the life rooted in genuine relationship that can transform our world. If we can love God, and know how to approach Him, then we can apply that revelation knowledge in dealing with ourselves. The world needs to learn from us on how to love. Exemplifying God is true Christianity.

Alfred Tagoe has done a brilliant job in this inspirational writing, it is well researched, and full of life. It will capture the interest of the average reader, illuminate the biblical Christian, and fine tune the biblical scholar. I highly recommend this book to all who desire to go deeper with God.

Dr. George Agbonson
Presiding Bishop, Global Ministers and Churches Alliance & Christ Restoration Ministries International

I have been friends with Alfred for a few years now. When I think of him, I think *"Alfred is a man after God's own heart"*. From the way he leads his church, his passionate intercession, to the kind of father he is—he shines with the love of Jesus. Alfred has written a book that he has lived. He is obsessed with Jesus and it shows on every page of this book. If you want a blueprint to greater intimacy, joy and communion with Jesus, this book will not disappoint.

Jim Baker
Lead Pastor, Zion Christian Center

PROLOGUE

INTIMACY! This Is a word that conjures up different emotions, passions, and even meaning, to different people. When this word is spoken the most prevalent thought that comes to mind has to do with sex. Many in our society equate intimacy with sex and vice-versa. This however could not be further from the truth.

Although in many cases intimacy may lead to sexual intercourse, in terms of human male and female interactions, it does not automatically however equate to sex. In fact, it is true that many sexual encounters are devoid of any intimacy. Two such examples are in the cases of prostitution and rape.

In prostitution, the sexual encounter is more of a "business" transaction where both parties engage in the act for very different reasons in order to fulfill their own individual selfish lusts. On one hand the prostitute does it to fulfill his or her monetary lust, while on the other hand the solicitor does it to fulfill his or her sexual desires. In each case, both parties do not really care about the other's real needs.

In the case of rape, ONLY perpetrators get what they want with no regard to the victim's desires or well-being, thus leaving the victim broken and scarred, sometimes for the rest of their life.

So, if intimacy is not the same as sex, what is it then? According to the dictionary, intimacy is defined as "a close, familiar, and usually affectionate or loving personal relationship with another person or group[1]". In other words, intimacy involves a deep familiarity between two parties that is founded on their love or affection for each other, a love that may not be shared with any other.

I have heard it also said in certain reputable circles that intimacy means *"Into-me-see"*. This definition connotes that intimacy involves a certain kind of transparency, oneness, and even vulnerability that benefits both parties in a relationship. It requires both parties to totally open themselves up by granting the other party exclusive access to their most inward secrets and denying entry to all others. When this happens, sex then becomes the consummation of that intimacy.

The truth is God specifically designated sexual intercourse to take place ONLY within the confines of a covenant marriage of love and partnership between one man and one woman (***Genesis 2:24 – 25***). In other words, God created sex to become the ultimate climax of intimacy between a man and his wife, and never intended for this experience to exist outside the confines of that covenant marriage relationship.

God is an intimate God who created you and me to be intimate beings in order to have an intimate relationship with Him, and with our spouse. Although, many are successful in intimacy with their spouse, they however, fail to be intimate with the creator of intimacy. God wants us to be passionate believers in hot pursuit after Him because we were created for His pleasure *(Revelation 4:11)*.

INTRODUCTION

The story of the Bible - from the Genesis of mankind in the Garden of Eden to his redemption after the fall, is a story of intimacy. This intimate love story between God and man is finally consummated in the Book of Revelation. Here we see God the Father presenting us - the redeemed and ransomed Church, as a Bride without spot or wrinkle to His Son our Bridegroom *(Rev. 21:9)*.

In fact, the Apostle Paul in his wonderful description of the purpose of marriage, and the roles of husbands and wives in Ephesians 5 confirms this remarkable desire of God to have intimacy with His people. As Paul admonishes husbands to love their wives, he compares it to the way Christ, our Bridegroom, loves His Bride the Church. As he concludes his remarks, he seems to be caught up in an intimate bliss with His Lover that makes him to understand that the real purpose of the visible marital covenant on earth is to express the intimacy that the invisible God wants to have with man.

Ephesians 5:25 – 32:

"Husbands, love your wives, just as Christ also loved the church and gave Himself for it … This is a great mystery, but I am speaking about Christ and the church."

The Garden of Eden

There are many who preach and teach that the Garden of Eden is the goal of our redemption. In other words, Jesus' death and resurrection was intended to return us to our original state in Eden where man's needs and wants were fully provided by God, and man had no need to struggle. As much as this assertion has an essence of truth, I believe it falls short of what Eden was intended to be.

So True!

God created man and put him in the Garden of Eden to have intimacy and communion with Him first and foremost. It was through this communion that man was also empowered to fulfill His other assignment of subduing and managing the earth. Through this awesome fellowship between Deity and humanity, man fully understood that his mandate was not only to enjoy all the benefits afforded him in the garden, but more importantly to extend the garden and its heavenly conditions beyond Eden.

As a result of Adam's intimacy experience with God in the Garden, he was also able to exercise dominion over all of God's other creatures. Once Adam chose to willingly disobey God's simple but direct command, however, he lost what was most important to him - his intimate communion with God. ~~Once he lost his communion, then he automatically also lost his dominion.~~ !) | *POWERFUL!!!*

After God created man and put him in Eden, the highlight of God's day was making regular visits with him to commune and fellowship in the cool of the day as intimacy partners, or ~~dare I say as co-equals.~~

Genesis 3:8 – 9:
*"And they heard the voice of the LORD God **walking in the garden in the cool of the day**: and Adam and his wife hid themselves from **the presence of the LORD God** amongst the trees of the garden. And the LORD God called unto Adam, and said unto him, **Where art thou?"***

adam + Eve partners

For the ~~first~~ time in their co-existence together as *we* partners, ~~Adam and his wife~~ missed their daily *don't know it was* appointment with God. I believe it was during these intimate encounters that God revealed to Adam all he *if* needed to know on how to manage the earth and all *his* the resources He had abundantly provided. ~~Our intimacy with God is the impetus through which we receive instruction and direction on how to manage our homes, churches, communities, businesses, and the nation(s).~~ *daily*

I can hear the agony in God's voice when He calls unto Adam, *"where are you?"*. His friend (and intimacy partner) was nowhere to be found. As a result of sin, Adam missed his ~~daily~~ appointment with God by hiding from His presence. Up until now God's presence had been his daily joy and delight. After Adam sinned, he now found himself naked and separated from that which was his perpetual covering. Adam allowed the devil to bring separation between him and his creator, thus depriving God of what He desired most - **INTIMACY!**

Understanding this truth will radically transform the way we perceive our salvation. Yes, God wants us to return to the Eden lifestyle and enjoy all His benefits of provision and protection. However, the primary reason Jesus died and was resurrected was to restore our communion and intimacy with the God-Head - God the Father, the Son, and the Holy Spirit. Once our communion with God is restored, then we will also rediscover our lost dominion. It is through our communion with God that we are able to fully take dominion over sin, sickness, depravity, death, and the devil himself.

The sad truth is that even after being saved and enjoying many of the benefits from our "redemption package", I believe many of us if we listen closely, will hear God calling unto us, *"Alfred, where are you?"*; or *"Sue, where are you?"*. Even though many of us are saved, we may not yet be where God intended for us to be, which is in the place of communion and intimacy with Him.

Just like Israel of old, it is unfortunate that many believers focus more on the benefits of their redemption - such as their health, provision, and even their opportunity to serve God and be used mightily by Him. Although the "Eden" experience is important, it should not however cause us to lose sight of one of the primary benefits of our personal salvation, which is to grant us intimacy with God.

The Exodus

Most of us, if not all, can recall the story of the exodus of God's people from Egyptian captivity into the Promised Land by God's mighty hand. Just like the Jews during that time, we usually tend to miss God's primary purpose in delivering His people from bondage. While the children of Israel were more focused on the Promised Land - a land flowing with milk and honey, God was more focused on bringing them to a place of intimacy and divine encounter with Him. Having a relationship and knowing the giver of the promise is always more important than just receiving the promise.

Before they would ever set their eyes and feet on the Promised Land it was important for the children of Israel to have their own personal encounter with God. God had to first bring them unto Himself, so that they would commune with Him. This was the initial phase of God's plan to restore mankind back to their original state of intimate fellowship with Him, just like in the Garden of Eden.

Unfortunately to God's chagrin, His chosen people would have nothing to do with His proposition. Just like it is today, the people were more interested in receiving God's promises than intimately walking with the Promise-Giver.

Exodus 19:3 – 6:
*"And Moses went up to God, and the LORD called to him from the mountain, saying, "Thus you shall say to the house of Jacob, and tell the children of Israel: 'You have seen what I did to the Egyptians, and how I bore you on eagles' wings and **brought you to Myself**. Now therefore, if you will indeed obey My voice and keep My covenant, then you shall be a special treasure to Me above all people; for all the earth is Mine. And you shall be to Me a kingdom of priests and a holy nation.' These are the words which you shall speak to the children of Israel.""*

God was excited to meet with the children of Israel on the Mount and instructed Moses to prepare them for this encounter. When the time came for the whole nation to draw near to God's presence however, they drew back. They instead requested that Moses their leader be the only one to go to God on their behalf and return with God's instructions. Instead of being excited to have an encounter with God that would produce an intimate relationship with Him, they were completely satisfied with choosing Moses as their go-between.

Exodus 19:10 – 11:
"Then the LORD said to Moses, "Go to the people and consecrate them today and tomorrow and let them wash their clothes. And let them be ready for the third

day. For on the third day the LORD will come down upon Mount Sinai in the sight of all the people¨

Deuteronomy 5:24 -30:
*"And you said: 'Surely the LORD our God has shown us His glory and His greatness, and we have heard His voice from the midst of the fire. We have seen this day that God speaks with man; yet he still lives. Now therefore, **why should we die?** For this great fire will consume us; if we hear the voice of the LORD our God anymore, then we shall die. For who is there of all flesh who has heard the voice of the living God speaking from the midst of the fire, as we have, and lived? **You go near and hear all that the LORD our God may say and tell us all that the LORD our God says to you, and we will hear and do it.'** "Then the LORD heard the voice of your words when you spoke to me, and the LORD said to me: 'I have heard the voice of the words of this people which they have spoken to you. They are right in all that they have spoken. **Oh, that they had such a heart in them that they would fear Me and always keep all My commandments,** that it might be well with them and with their children forever! Go and say to them, "**Return to your tents**""".*

Can you sense the disappointment in God's heart when He responded to the people's excuses about why they could not come close to Him? God had prepared Himself like a bridegroom to meet His bride, but unfortunately His bride was not prepared to meet Him. He wanted them to know Him, so that they would be empowered to obey His commands and walk in all that He had in store for them. Their greatest purpose, however, would be that through their encounter with God, they would become just like Him and reflect His glory to the rest of the surrounding nations. Since the children of Israel chose to worship God from afar and refused to have an intimate relationship with Him, God had no choice but to allow only Moses unlimited access to His presence.

Unlike the rest of the children of Israel, Moses refused to enter the Promised Land without God's presence. Instead, he preferred to stay in the dreary wilderness with the presence, rather than go into the land flowing with milk and honey without it.

Exodus 33:15 – 17:
"Then he said to Him, "If Your Presence does not go with us, do not bring us up from here. For how then will it be known that Your people and I have found grace in Your sight, except You go with us? So we shall be separate, Your people and I, from all the people who are upon the face of the earth." So the LORD said to Moses, "I will also do this thing that you have spoken; for you have found grace in My sight, and I know you by name.""

Moses fully understood that having an intimate relationship with God was far more important and rewarding than just possessing the Promised Land. Are you more satisfied with having the gifts and promises of God, even if it means not having His presence with you in a vibrant way? Do you pursue His presents more than having His presence; or are you like Moses who refused to live without His presence?

Since the children of Israel refused to embrace their corporate destiny as a nation of Priests, God decided to separate the tribe of Levi for this unique assignment. Aaron and his four sons were the first priests appointed by God, with Aaron serving as the High Priest. Their priestly role was to minister before the Lord and offer sacrifices on behalf of the people *(See Exodus 28)*.

Just like the nation of Israel was called to be a kingdom of priests, today we as the Body of Christ also have a similar calling to be a kingdom of priests. As priests of the Most-High God therefore, our primary function is to minister before the Lord, then reflect His character and virtues to the world around us. The Apostle Peter confirms this when he says:

1 Peter 2:5 & 9:
*"You also, as living stones, are being built up a spiritual house, **a holy priesthood**, to offer up spiritual sacrifices acceptable to God through Jesus Christ...But you are a chosen generation, **a royal priesthood**, a holy nation, His own special people, **that you may proclaim the praises of Him** who called you out of darkness into His marvelous light."*

Furthermore, God instituted a system of worship for His people and established a pattern for how they would approach Him. This systematic approach would not only guide the nation of Israel for generations but would also serve as a shadow for how we as born-again children of God would access His throne in order to walk in perpetual intimacy.

God revealed this pattern to Moses while he was visiting with Him on the mountain and fasting for forty days and nights. During Moses' visitation, God not only revealed the Throne Room from the heavenly Temple, but also asked Moses to replicate what he saw on earth. During his encounter with God the Tabernacle of Moses was also unveiled to him and Moses was commanded to build this Tabernacle in Wilderness where the children of Israel would encounter God. He was also given specific instructions concerning its design, dimensions, and articles - which are enumerated in Exodus chapters 25 through 28.

The Tabernacle of Moses

There were essentially two main sections within the Tabernacle - the Outer Court and the Inner Court. The Inner Court, however, also had two sections which were divided by a veil, namely the Holy Place and the Most Holy Place. Therefore, the Tabernacle had three separate areas overall - the Outer Court, the Holy Place, and the Most Holy Place, which was also known as the Holy of Holies.

There were also unique articles of furniture specifically designated for each area of the Tabernacle. Each piece of furniture had a specific role in the systematic and progressive worship of the people. It is important to reiterate that Moses did not come up

~~with his own idea on how the tabernacle had to be built but received specific instructions on what and how the tabernacle had to be constructed.~~

Exodus 26:30 – 36:
*"And you shall raise up the tabernacle according to its pattern which you were shown on the mountain." You shall make a veil woven of blue, purple, and scarlet thread, and fine woven linen... And you shall hang the veil from the clasps. Then you shall bring the ark of the Testimony in there, behind the veil. **The veil shall be a divider for you between the holy place and the Most Holy.** You shall put the mercy seat upon the ark of the Testimony in the Most Holy. You shall set the table outside the veil, and the lampstand across from the table on the side of the tabernacle toward the south; and you shall put the table on the north side. "You shall make a screen for the door of the tabernacle, woven of blue, purple, and scarlet thread, and fine woven linen, made by a weaver."*

Our Lord and Savior Jesus Christ came to fulfill every significant detail of the Tabernacle. He offers us a fresh perspective on how to return to our original purpose of intimacy with God by providing an understanding of the ancient pattern of worship God revealed to His servant Moses. We will be discussing this in more detail in the proceeding chapters by highlighting how each area of the Tabernacle applies to our walk of intimacy with God today.

SECTION ONE

JESUS, THE WAY
JESUS, MY SAVIOR
JESUS, OUR JUSTIFICATION

CHAPTER 1

I AM THE WAY, THE TRUTH, AND THE LIFE

The scriptures clearly reveal that Jesus came to fulfill the Old Testament's requirements for following God. On several occasions Jesus also declared this as well.

Matthew 5:17:
"Do not think that I came to destroy the Law or the Prophets. I did not come to destroy but to fulfill."

Jesus' greatest assignment in coming to earth was to die for you and me. As a result of His death, Jesus fulfilled all the necessary requirements to reposition us back on the right track to pursue intimate fellowship with God. The personal communion and intimacy Adam lost in the Garden of Eden - as a result of sin, could now be properly restored between God the Father and mankind.

Hebrews 9:1 – 12:
"Then indeed, even the first covenant had ordinances of divine service and the earthly sanctuary. For a tabernacle was prepared: the first part, in which was the lampstand, the table, and the showbread, which is called the sanctuary; and behind the second veil, the part of the tabernacle which is called the Holiest of All, which had the golden censer and the ark of the covenant overlaid on all sides with gold, in which were the golden pot that had the manna, Aaron's rod that budded, and the tablets of the covenant; and above it were the cherubim of glory overshadowing the mercy seat. Of these things we cannot now speak in detail. Now when these things had been thus prepared, the priests always went into the first part of the tabernacle, performing the services. But into the second part the high priest went alone once a year, not without blood, which he offered for himself and for the people's sins committed in ignorance; the **Holy Spirit indicating this, that the way into the Holiest of All was not yet made manifest while the first tabernacle was still standing. It was symbolic for the present time** *... But Christ came as High Priest of the good things to come, with the greater and more perfect tabernacle not made with hands, that is, not of this creation. Not with the blood of goats and calves, but with His own blood He entered the Most Holy Place once for all, having obtained eternal redemption."*

As this remarkable scripture portrays, Jesus is the personification and divine fulfillment of everything associated with the Tabernacle, including all its articles, processes, and symbolisms. Furthermore, in one of His final discourses with His disciples, Jesus boldly revealed to them His identity and His assignment.

John 14:6:
"Jesus said to him, "I am the way, the truth, and the life. No one comes to the Father except through Me".

I believe this scripture to be one of the boldest statements Jesus ever made concerning who He was during His earthly ministry. It has tremendous implications which have created much controversy in various religious circles. In both ancient and current times, many people worldwide would love to make Christians believe there are many ways to access God through other religions, and that all roads lead to heaven. Jesus' statement, however, categorically dismisses both assertions as false claims. With this declaration, Jesus cancelled all doubts and settled every counterfeit claim by deliberately using the definite article **"the"** to describe Himself as the only pathway to encounter the one true and living God.

When Jesus' Jewish audience heard His statement, they immediately understood He was referring to the Temple, which was designed and built after the pattern of the Tabernacle of Moses. This was not a new concept, as on many other occasions Jesus referenced His mission on earth in correlation with the Temple.

For example, in the Gospel of John, Chapter 2, Jesus spoke concerning His death and resurrection in reference to the Temple:

John 2:19 – 21:
"Jesus answered and said to them, "Destroy this temple, and in three days I will raise it up." Then the Jews said, "It has taken forty-six years to build this temple, and will You raise it up in three days?" But He was speaking of the temple of His body."

Therefore, when Jesus said to His disciples that *"I am the Way, the Truth, and the Life"*, they would have immediately understood that He was referring to the three sections of the Temple. In essence, Jesus was drawing His audience's attention to the fact that everything they understood about the Temple and its process of worship began and ended with Him. After all He is the ALPHA and the OMEGA!

Jesus' remarkable statement raises unique questions about our relationship with Him and how He desires for us to approach God. What does it mean to us that He is *"the Way, the Truth, and the Life"*? This will be discussed further in the following sections.

Jesus also emphasized the importance of the sequential approach to encounter God the Father, when He says, *"no one comes to the Father except through me"*. I sincerely believe Jesus was making it crystal clear that no one will have a vibrant intimate relationship with the Father, EXCEPT they first encounter Him as the Way, then as the Truth, and finally as the Life in that sequential order.

Since intimacy with the Father should be the Christian's highest goal, understanding this process of how to approach our Lord is paramount. This is our journey of intimacy with the Father. In the following sections therefore, we will explore various aspects of Jesus' statement to His disciples in relation to Moses' Tabernacle. We will discover how they apply to us today in our quest to encounter God through intimacy in order to fulfill our destiny in Christ.

In Section I, we will explore **Jesus as the Way** in relation to the Outer Court of the Tabernacle, and how this applies to our salvation experience in Christ. In Section II, we will explore **Jesus as the Truth** in relation to the Holy Place, and how it applies to our sanctification experience in Christ. Finally, in Section III we will explore **Jesus as the Life** in relation to the Most Holy Place, and how this applies to our superior joy in Christ.

May you enjoy this journey as you discover how to grow in intimacy with God as your Creator, Father, and Bridegroom. God is eagerly waiting to grant you a lifetime of unlimited personal encounters with Him in His presence - are you ready? Let us begin!!!

CHAPTER 2

THE OUTER COURT

As we begin our journey into intimacy with God through the Tabernacle of Moses, the first place we come to is the Outer Court. The most significant item in this area is the Brazen Altar. This is where all the sacrifices for the people and nation took place. The Priests would slay the various sacrificial animals and spill their blood for the remission of the people's sins. Once a year on the Day of Atonement, one male lamb was slaughtered on this Altar and its blood spilled. Some of the blood was then taken by the High Priest to the Holy of Holies to be sprinkled on the Mercy Seat. This represented the atonement and forgiveness of the nation's sins.

Jesus fulfilled the requirements of our salvation when He became the supreme sacrificial lamb to be slaughtered on our behalf. As a result, His blood was shed as the ultimate price for the remission of our sins. It is interesting in this context that Jesus is also the High-Priest who took His very own blood and sprinkled it on the Mercy Seat in the Heavenly Temple for our justification and redemption.

Hebrews 9:11 – 12:

"But when Christ appeared as a high priest of the good things that have come, then through the greater and more perfect tent (not made with hands, that is, not of this creation) he entered once for all into the holy places, not by means of the blood of goats and calves but by means of his own blood, thus securing an eternal redemption."

Jesus is **the Way** because He paved the way for our redemption, so that you and I can begin our journey back to the Father through intimacy. In other words, the entrance or gate to the Outer Court can be referred to as **The Way**. In fact, it is interesting to note that before the first century church believers were called "Christians" in Acts 11, they were first referred to as the people *"of the Way"*, which signified that they were recognized by others as the disciples who knew **the Way** to salvation.

Acts 9:1 – 2:

"Then Saul, still breathing threats and murder against the disciples of the Lord, went to the high priest and asked letters from him to the synagogues

*of Damascus, so that if he found any **who were of the Way**, whether men or women, he might bring them bound to Jerusalem."*

You cannot begin your journey of intimacy with the Father without first encountering Jesus as **the Way**. This is the Outer Court experience; where Jesus sheds His blood, becomes your sacrificial lamb, and ultimately your Savior. This is the place of justification; where you and I become justified - just as if we never sinned, through the blood of Jesus and receive His righteousness. This experience occurs when you and I receive Jesus into our hearts and become born again into the family of God.

John 3:3 & 7:
*"Jesus answered and said to him, "Most assuredly, I say to you, **unless one is born again, he cannot see the kingdom of God.**" Do not marvel that I said to you, '**You must be born again.**'"*

John 1:12 – 13:
"But as many as received Him, to them He gave the right to become children of God, to those who believe in His name: who were born, not of blood, nor of the will of the flesh, nor of the will of man, but of God."

If you have already received Jesus into your heart as Lord and Savior, then you have encountered Him as **the Way**. You have therefore begun your journey into intimacy with the Father through His Son. If, however, you have not yet accepted Jesus and the price He paid for your redemption on the cross of Calvary, then you are still outside of God's covenant of grace and are unable to access the promise of intimacy with your creator. You are therefore also missing out on all the marvelous rewards that intimacy with the Godhead will afford you.

If you are not a born-again Christian I would like to pause right now and allow you to take the first step into this remarkable journey of intimacy with God by receiving Jesus into your heart as your personal Lord and Savior. Just repeat this simple prayer:

Dear Jesus, I come to you just as I am; I acknowledge that I am a sinner in need of a Savior. I believe with my heart that You died for my sin and that God raised you up on the third day for my justification. I therefore confess you to be my Lord and my Savior. Cleanse me with your precious blood and help me to know you more and more in a real way. Thank you for the opportunity to begin a journey of intimacy with my Father through You. Amen!

If you prayed this prayer with sincerity, then your journey into intimacy with God has begun and your life is about to be radically changed as you pursue Him with your whole heart. Find a good bible-based church that believes and teaches the word of God and that will help you grow in your walk, and fellowship with other like-minded believers. Read your bible every opportunity you have and pray every day. As you continue to read this book, you will also learn many practical and spiritual principles to assist you in your glorious journey of intimacy the Father has prepared for you. May God help you to finish your course!

CHAPTER 3

LITTLE CHILDREN

Just as in our natural process of growth we begin as children, then move on to young adults, then finally adulthood. The same is true in our spiritual maturity. John the Apostle clearly describes these three stages, or levels of growth in 1 John 2:12 – 14:

1 John 2:12 – 14:
"I am writing to you, little children, because your sins are forgiven for his name's sake. I am writing to you, fathers, because you know him who is from the beginning. I am writing to you, young men, because you have overcome the evil one. I write to you, children, because you know the Father. I write to you, fathers, because you know him who is from the beginning. I write to you, young men, because you

are strong, and the word of God abides in you, and
you have overcome the evil one."

Since our journey of intimacy with God through the various areas of the Tabernacle corresponds to our level of maturity in the Lord, we will also discuss what stage of maturity is highlighted in each of the three areas, beginning with the Outer Court.

Once we receive Jesus as the Way into our lives and become born again, we are considered children of God. We have only begun the journey to encounter God in intimacy and all He has in store for us. It is indeed wonderful that many have made it into the Outer Court of this journey, and received the salvation purchased for them by Jesus as the blood of the Lamb. God, however, never intended for you and me to remain in the Outer Court as children, but to mature and take the next steps of pursuing intimacy with God.

There are a few comparisons that can be gleaned from the Outer Court experience and the characteristics of a newborn child in the kingdom of God. Firstly, those who remain in the Outer Court as children are those who still have a sin-consciousness. These believers focus on their sin nature, and inadvertently continue to yield to its desires. Although most of these Christians are sincere, many of them are immature, and in need of reassurance of God's love and forgiveness. As a result of their immaturity and sin-consciousness, they are also very susceptible to the enemy's accusations through shame, guilt, and condemnation. The Apostle John addressed this group of believers in his Epistle to the Church:

1 John 2:1 & 12:
*"My little children, these things I write to you, so that you may not sin. And if anyone sins, we have an Advocate with the Father, Jesus Christ the righteous... I write to you, **little children, because your sins are forgiven you for His name's sake.**"*

As previously mentioned, if you find yourself experiencing a great deal of shame and condemnation because of sin in your life; and you also constantly need to be reassured of God's love and forgiveness, these are characteristics of little children according to the Apostle John.

The Issue of the Flesh

The reason why most people continue to remain in this Outer Court mentality, which is filled with sin-consciousness, is that they continue to walk according to their carnal mind and their flesh. You see in the Outer Court; the main source of illumination is natural sun light. This also signifies that those who operate in this area only rely on their natural senses of sight, sound, smell, and touch. These believers are guided by their own sense of right and wrong. These immature saints therefore invariably end up fulfilling the lust of their flesh, rather than fulfilling the righteous requirement of the law through the Spirit.

The Apostle Paul had a lot to say about this phenomenon throughout his Epistles to the Churches. He admonished the saints to grow into maturity and advance from their status as little children in the Outer Court. He, however, reserved his greatest admonition to the Corinthian church. Although the Corinthians operated in the gifts of the Spirit - perhaps more than all the other churches, Paul still considered them infants in their walk with the Lord because they were carnally minded instead of being spiritually minded. In other words, they relied on their five natural senses more than their spiritual senses in their relationship with the Lord.

1 Corinthians 3:1 – 3:
*"And I, brethren, could not speak to you as to spiritual people but as **to carnal, as to babes in Christ**. I fed you with milk and not with solid food; for until now you were not able to receive it, and even now you are still not able; **for you are still carnal**. For where there are envy, strife, and divisions among you, are you not carnal and behaving like mere men?"*

Romans 8:5 – 8:
*"**For those who live according to the flesh set their minds on the things of the flesh**, but those who live according to the Spirit, the things of the Spirit. For to be carnally minded is death, but to be spiritually minded is life and peace. Because the carnal mind is enmity against God; for it is not subject to the law of God, nor indeed can be. **So then, those who are in the flesh cannot please God.**"*

Fatal Distractions

One of the most common characteristics of little children is that they are easily distracted by the occurrences in their environment. This is very much the case for those spiritual children in their Outer Court experience with the Lord. You see there is so much activity that goes on in the Outer Court, which distracts us from seriously focusing on the Lord. Let's remember that it was in the Outer Court that Jesus made a whip, overturned the tables of the money changers, and drove out all those that bought and sold animals in the Temple *(See Matthew 21:12)*. Can you imagine anyone trying to seriously focus on God in such an environment?

The truth is those who remain children in the Outer Court are those who are easily tossed to and fro by natural circumstances and the cares of this life. They are controlled by their natural senses more than their spiritual senses. In other words, they fall prey to walking by their sight and not by their faith, which is contrary to what the bible instructs us to do. According to 2 Corinthians 5:7 we are to *"walk by faith, not by sight"*.

Open Rebellion

There are some Christians in the Outer Court experience who have encountered Jesus as both their Savior and the Way, but they have not fully realized that they have been justified through His blood. These believers, therefore, continue to live in open rebellion toward God, and often use a perverted grace message to justify their lifestyle of sin. Consequently, by doing so, they seek to crucify the Lord of Glory repeatedly.

The Apostle Paul cautions us who have begun the journey of intimacy with the Father not to just settle in the Outer Court and willfully continue in our sins.

Hebrews 10:26 – 29:
*"For **if we sin willfully** after we have received the knowledge of the truth, there no longer remains a sacrifice for sins, but a certain fearful expectation of judgment, and fiery indignation which will devour the adversaries. Anyone who has rejected Moses' law dies without mercy on the testimony of two or three witnesses. Of how much worse punishment, do you suppose, will he be thought worthy who has trampled the Son of God underfoot, counted the blood of the covenant by which he was sanctified a common thing, and **insulted the Spirit of grace?"***

For those sincere believers who still struggle to appreciate and walk in the justification of the Lord Jesus, and are constantly being bombarded by the devil to feel guilty, ashamed, and condemned, Paul delivers a word of assurance:

Romans 8:1 & 2:
*"There is therefore now **no condemnation** to those who are in Christ Jesus, who do not walk according to the flesh, but according to the Spirit. For the law of the Spirit of life in Christ Jesus has made me free from the law of sin and death".*

This wonderful encouragement, however, is for those sincere believers who *"do not walk according to the flesh"*. This means they are not satisfied with only an Outer Court experience of knowing that Jesus is the Way, and that they have been saved and justified by His blood. They are yearning for more. Their gaze is set to experience everything Jesus accomplished on their behalf through the shedding of His blood on the cross of Calvary. They are also intent to know Him as the Truth and the Life, and to grow into maturity and intimacy with the Father through His Son. For these believers, the *Brazen Altar* ceases to be the focal point of their experience.

As they prepare to enter the second phase of their growth and intimacy with God in the Holy Place, their attention is drawn to the *Brazen Laver* - which is situated a few yards from the *Brazen Altar*. The *Brazen Laver* is a symbol of their desire to submit to God's sanctification process of transforming them from "little children" to "young adults"; and from a life of little fruit, to one of more fruit. We will discuss this process further in Section Two.

CHAPTER 4

FRUIT OF REPENTANCE

In 1994 my family and I went to the United Kingdom (U.K.) to visit my brother and some extended family members. This was during a tumultuous period of my life as I was going through a spiritual crisis. I was engaged in a spiritual battle with demonic oppression and depression, while at the same time feeling a pull by God to encounter Him in a way I had never experienced. In all honesty, having been raised in a deeply religious and traditional background, I did not know what I was dealing with, and how to seek freedom from this onslaught from Hell. This trip to London, nevertheless, began to change everything.

While in London I was exposed to two expressions of church life. When I was with the first set of relatives, we attended the Church of England - which is very similar to the Anglican Church. It was a beautiful Cathedral with its stain glass windows, crystal chandeliers, beautiful saint statues, and mostly empty padded pews. Although I was very familiar with the monotonous liturgical worship and had been around this type of atmosphere most of my life, during this trip it truly felt dead and empty. For the first time something was not right. There was nothing to suggest the people even expected God to move in their lives, let alone answer their prayers.

What was even more alarming was that while the pews were relatively empty in this gorgeous edifice, the nearby soccer stadium was quickly filling up on this cold Sunday morning with throngs of people ready to watch the *Tottenham Hotspurs FC* soccer match that afternoon. Although I still could not understand everything that was going on, I knew down on the inside that something was not right with this picture.

I spent the following week staying with another cousin who, unlike me and the family I had just been with, was a Pentecostal Christian and attended a non-denominational Pentecostal church where shouting in praise, hand clapping, and speaking in tongues was the norm. Although I initially felt a little awkward during this Pentecostal service, I also could not avoid recognizing the difference in this church's expression of joy and faith compared to the congregation I visited the previous Sunday. The décor of the Pentecostal church was not at all elaborate; needless to say, it was nothing to write home about. There was however an overwhelming exuberance that filled the atmosphere, and a definite tangible presence that could be felt in their worship. After the service, my cousin introduced me to the pastor. While meeting with him privately he answered some of my lingering questions and addressed several doubts I had about God and my faith.

After leaving London and returning home to Ghana, something was very different. I began to feel a breakthrough from the tug of war in my spirit, and I finally surrendered my life to Jesus and became a part of the Pentecostal Charismatic movement. Although I was still engaged in warfare with the enemy, I could sense I was breaking ground and gaining the upper hand as I drew closer to God through prayer and the Word.

The Lord also began to give me tremendous insight into His Word. In prayer and study one day, He referenced my experience in London with the fig tree that had leaves but lacked fruit. Although you can find this account in all the Synoptic Gospels (Matthew, Mark, and Luke), I would like to focus your attention on the account in the Gospel of Mark:

Mark 11:12 – 14:
*"On the following day, when they came from Bethany, **he was hungry**. And seeing in the distance a fig tree in leaf, he went to see if he could find anything on it. When he came to it, he found **nothing but leaves**, for it was not the season for figs. And he*

*said to it, "May no one ever eat fruit from you again."
And his disciples heard it."*

This episode in the life of Jesus has been used extensively to teach on faith in most church circles. During my encounter with the Lord, however, He used it rather to show me what the church and the Christian life should look like. When God looks at the church, what does He see? When people look at the church - what do they see, and what do they receive? When they look at you as a Christian - what do they see from afar, and what do they actually experience once they come up close? Will they see just leaves, or will they see fruit? You see Jesus was attracted to the fig tree because of the leaves, but what He needed to satisfy His hunger was fruit, not leaves.

Thank God for our religious leaves, such as our beautiful houses of worship and all the other wonderful things we do in church. These things, however, will not satisfy the heart of God, and most definitely will never quench the hungry and thirsty soul of lost humanity. Unfortunately, many Churches and Christians put more emphasis on the form of religion but deny the power thereof. The Apostle Paul accurately described the characteristics of people in these last days in 2 Timothy 3:5:

2 Timothy 3:5:
"...having the appearance of godliness but denying its power."

Like the Pharisees and Priests, who were the religious leaders of Jesus' day, these churches also prefer to look the part on the outside, but not be the part on the inside. They would rather focus on maintaining the upkeep of their outward appearance and reputation, more so than developing their inward character and personal integrity. Jesus reserved most of His chastisement for these leaders and called them *"whitewashed tombs full of dead men's bones"*. He made it very clear that producing fruit was more important than maintaining leaves by stating – *"they shall know you by your fruit"*. Church it's time to stop **playing** church, and actually time to rise up and **be** the church.

Matthew 23:26 – 28:
"You blind Pharisee! First clean the inside of the cup and the plate, that the outside also may be clean. "Woe to you, scribes and Pharisees, hypocrites! For you are like whitewashed tombs, which outwardly appear beautiful, but within are full of dead people's bones and all uncleanness. So you also outwardly appear righteous to others, but within you are full of hypocrisy and lawlessness."

Matthew 7:15 – 20:
*"... You will **recognize them by their fruits**. Are grapes gathered from thorn bushes, or figs from thistles? So, every healthy tree bears good fruit, but the diseased tree bears bad fruit. A healthy tree cannot bear bad fruit, nor can a diseased tree bear good fruit. Every tree that does not bear good fruit is*

cut down and thrown into the fire. **Thus, you will recognize them by their fruits.**"

Fruitfulness is a very important principle of the Christian faith. Bearing fruit has been the goal of the Father from the very beginning of creation when He blessed the first couple and commanded them to - *"be fruitful, and multiply, and replenish the earth, and subdue it: and have dominion..."* **(Gen. 1:28).**

In John 15, Jesus speaks extensively about the concept of intimacy. In this passage we find one of His most important discourses with the disciples before His Passion experience leading up to the cross. Jesus is deliberating with His disciples about the importance of abiding in Him. **Abiding** meant they were to learn how to stay intimately connected to Him, just like a branch stays intimately connected to its vine in order to receive life. He stated unequivocally that the main purpose for their abiding in Him was so that they could bear fruit. As I stated earlier, it is our communion with God that produces our dominion over the earth. Furthermore, without intimacy there cannot be fruit, because after all fruitfulness flows from intimacy.

John 15:1 – 8:
*""I am the true vine, and My Father is the vinedresser. Every branch in Me that does not bear fruit He takes away; and **every branch that bears fruit** He prunes, that it may **bear more fruit.** You are already clean because of the word which I have spoken to you. Abide in Me, and I in you. As the*

branch cannot bear fruit of itself, unless it abides in the vine, neither can you, unless you abide in Me. "I am the vine; you are the branches. He who abides in Me, and I in him, bears much fruit; for without Me you can do nothing... If you abide in Me, and My words abide in you, you will ask what you desire, and it shall be done for you. By this My Father is glorified, that you **bear much fruit***; so, you will be My disciples"* (Emphasis mine)

Also, in John 15, Jesus speaks of three levels of fruitfulness that I believe relate to the three levels of intimacy we will be discussing throughout this book. The three levels of fruitfulness are - *fruit*, *more fruit*, and *much fruit*.

As you and I grow in our journey of intimacy from the Outer Court to the Holy of Holies, we also increase in our ability to bear fruit in the Kingdom of God. We will describe the types of fruit God wants us to bear at each level of intimacy as we encounter Jesus as the Way, the Truth, and the Life.

The first level of fruitfulness as described in John 15 is **fruit**, or "some fruit". I believe that as we encounter Jesus as the Way in the Outer Court, there is **some fruit** He expects us to bear.

As we have already seen, we enter the Outer Court through the door of repentance in order to receive forgiveness for our sins. It is unfortunate that in today's church, the word "repentance" is treated like a "cuss" word; never to be uttered from the pulpit for fear that a seeker-sensitive, politically correct generation will be offended and leave the church. We have diluted the requirements necessary for true conversion so much so that it has diminished the role of repentance. This has left us raising a cross-less generation with unrepentant hearts who live in a godless world. It is important to bring the message of repentance back into the vocabulary of our churches and make it a foundational part of our sermons; just like we do the message of prosperity and healing.

Repentance is what gets you through the door. More importantly, an attitude of repentance is what will sustain your focus on the ultimate prize of the high calling of God in Christ Jesus - which is to become like Him. Repentance is neither a bad word, nor a negative thing. In fact, the Apostle Paul helps us to understand that it is the goodness of God that brings us to repentance.

Romans 2:4:
"Or do you despise the riches of His goodness, forbearance, and longsuffering, not knowing that the goodness of God leads you to repentance?"

It is sad to say that many people misconstrue the blessings of the Lord in their life or ministry as an automatic sign of God's approval of them, even though they continue to live a blatant immoral lifestyle. What they fail to realize is that God is using His goodness to woo them to a place of repentance – where they have a change of mind concerning their lifestyle, so they can return to the place where God wants them to be. The

Greek word for change of heart or mind is "metanoia". In the New Testament "metanoia" is commonly translated as repentance. Instead of referring to guilt, regret, and shame, this type of repentance however implies "to make a decision to turn around, and to face a new direction"[2]. A repentant heart is truly one of the greatest attributes Christians should have considering this characteristic is what draws us closer and closer to God. The more I see Him, the more I recognize how far away I am from becoming like Him. This causes me to have a change of heart and mind to pursue Him even more. In other words, repentance is not just reserved for the blatant sinner, but also for all who recognize that no matter how far along they may have come in their walk with the Lord, there is always room for them to grow more Christ-like.

Once we transition into the Outer Court and experience the benefits of the sacrificial blood shed for the remission of our sins, we should also recognize that we have been transported from the kingdom of darkness into the kingdom of light. Since we are no longer children of darkness or disobedience, we are also no longer subject to the desires of sin. As a result of this experience, we must begin to bear the fruit of repentance. This means that what began as a new attitude of the heart and a new decision of the mind, has to now become evident for all to see.

The first person to use the phrase "fruit of repentance" in the bible was John the Baptist. He was also the one who began his ministry preaching the Gospel of Repentance, and performing a Baptism of

Repentance, long before Jesus came on the scene. It is worth noting that Jesus also began His ministry preaching the same message of repentance. Jesus also put His stamp of approval on John's ministry by allowing John to baptize Him, even though He was without sin.

Matthew 3:1 – 8:

"In those days John the Baptist came preaching in the wilderness of Judea, and saying, "Repent, for the kingdom of heaven is at hand!"...Then Jerusalem, all Judea, and all the region around the Jordan went out to him and were baptized by him in the Jordan, confessing their sins. But when he saw many of the Pharisees and Sadducees coming to his baptism, he said to them, "Brood of vipers! Who warned you to flee from the wrath to come? **Therefore, bear fruits worthy of repentance***"*

According to John, bearing the fruit of repentance meant his captive audience had to begin to live differently from their lifestyle prior to their baptism of repentance. The baptism itself was not enough. Once we become saved there must also be a visible change that is consistent and congruent with the norms of the new Kingdom that we have now become a part of, which is the Kingdom of Heaven.

It is sad and unfortunate that in some Christian circles today, there seems to be no expectation or demand from sinners who get saved to have a change of attitude and behavior from their former lifestyle to a lifestyle that actually glorifies God. There is a song we used to sing back in Africa when I got saved that highlights this attitude of repentance and its corresponding fruit. The song went like this:

"Great change since I met Christ, great change since I met Christ, great change since I met Christ; there is a great change since I met Christ. The things I used to do, I do them no more; the things I used to say, I say them no more; the places I used to go, I go there no more; there is a great change since I met Christ" (Sony Okunson, "Great Change").

This should be the response of everyone who encounters Jesus as the Way in the Outer Court. When we receive His sacrifice as the burnt offering for our sin, we determine in our hearts to turn from our wicked ways in order to embrace a new way of life that glorifies God, and ushers us into a new experience with our wonderful Savior.

Some may argue that the issue of repentance from sin is really not a New Testament requirement for salvation. They may claim that when John the Baptist and Jesus declared for their hearers to repent, they did so while still under the Old Testament Law, not to mention their audience was Jewish and not Gentile. A careful review of the New Testament, however, reveals that the early Apostles - including Peter and Paul, made repentance a central theme of their salvation message to both Jews and Gentiles alike.

In fact, the very first message the Apostle Peter preached after the initiation of the Church dispensation on the Day of Pentecost included a call to repentance. When the Jews who had come to Jerusalem from all over the world heard Peter's exhortation, they wanted to know what they had to do to be saved. Peter did not mince words in his response to their question:

Acts 2:38:
*"And Peter said to them, "**Repent** and be baptized every one of you in the name of Jesus Christ for the forgiveness of your sins, and you will receive the gift of the Holy Spirit."*

What about the Gentiles? Was there also a requirement for them to repent? Yes, there absolutely was according to Paul, the Apostle to the Gentiles.

In one of his most powerful sermons ever to be recorded, Paul laid out God's requirement for salvation for all mankind, including both Jews and Gentiles. He explained to the Stoic philosophers in Athens that before the advent of Jesus' death and resurrection, God ignored the sins of the people due to their ignorance, but now required all men (and women) to repent and be saved:

Acts 17:30 – 31:
*"The times of ignorance God overlooked, but **now** he **commands all people everywhere to repent**, because he has fixed a day on which he will judge the world in righteousness by a man whom he has*

appointed; and of this he has given assurance to all by raising him from the dead.""

Furthermore, during his trial before King Agrippa, the Apostle Paul recounted his own salvation encounter with the Lord Jesus Christ, and the assignment he was given. It was because of his obedience to this assignment that he suffered so much hardship and cruelty, even from his own people. His assignment was to preach the Gospel to the Gentiles and require them to repent and bear the fruits of repentance.

Acts 26:19 – 20:
*"Therefore, O King Agrippa, I was not disobedient to the heavenly vision, but declared first to those in Damascus, then in Jerusalem and throughout all the region of Judea, and **also to the Gentiles**, that they **should repent** and turn to God, **performing deeds in keeping with their repentance** ..."*

Finally, according to the writer of the Book of Hebrews, *"repentance from dead works"* is one of the most fundamental doctrines of New Testament theology. As previously mentioned, it is in fact the starting point of our journey into intimacy with God.

Hebrews 6:1:
*"Therefore, let us leave the elementary doctrine of Christ and go on to maturity, not laying again a **foundation of repentance from dead works and of faith toward God**..."*

You see repentance - which means to have a change of mind or attitude towards one's sin, and to turn towards God, is a necessary requirement for salvation. The proof of repentance, however, is the fruit we bear after we make the decision to repent in our heart. Repentance always begins as a decision but is not fully consummated until there is a visible action taken as a result of the decision. In other words, what begins inwardly as a decision should manifest outwardly as an action that aligns with the new direction we have chosen.

There is a marvelous illustration of this principle in the bible. In the Gospel of Luke chapter 15, Jesus gave a parable about a father and his two sons. In this parable, known in Christian circles as the story of the "Prodigal Son", the younger son one day demanded his inheritance from his father. The father obliged and apportioned to both sons their inheritance. The younger son left home with his newfound wealth and squandered it on riotous living. When he run out of resources, he volunteered to work in a pig farm in order to shelter himself with the pigs and was even tempted to eat their food. After a while, the Bible says,

Luke 15:17 – 18:
"But when he came to himself, he said, 'How many of my father's hired servants have more than enough bread, but I perish here with hunger! I will arise and go to my father, and I will say to him, "Father, I have sinned against heaven and before you".

In other words, when he came to the realization that the path that he was on was totally out of the will of his father, he made a quality decision to return home to his father. However, the most important thing he did was to follow through with that decision by returning home. That is the process of repentance in a nutshell. Unfortunately, there are many people who even though they realize they are on the wrong path, and have a desire to change, however never follow through with those desires. It reminds me of the age-old saying, "the road to hell is paved with good intentions". Where repentance is concerned, "the thought alone does not count". It always must be followed with action!

Fruit of Righteousness

It is necessary to note that another term used in the New Testament to describe the fruit of repentance, is the fruit of righteousness. The latter term is used more frequently than the former in the New Testament. The Apostle Paul used "the fruit of righteousness" in his letters much in the same way that John the Baptist used "the fruit of repentance". In other words, Paul expected every new convert who had accepted the price of the cross to repent of their sins and put their faith in the Lord Jesus Christ. According to Paul, the new convert had to have both. They had to be in good standing with God – which is the gift of righteousness, and they also had to demonstrate right living before God – which is the fruit of righteousness.

Romans 6:13:
"Do not yield your members as instruments of unrighteousness to sin, but yield yourselves to God, as one alive from the dead, and your members as instruments of righteousness to God."

Philippians 1:10 – 11:
*"...that you may distinguish between things that differ, that you may be sincere and without offense until the day of Jesus Christ, being filled with the **fruits of righteousness** through Jesus Christ, to the glory and praise of God."*

Hebrews 12:11:
*"Now chastening for the present does not seem to be joyous, but grievous. Nevertheless, afterward it yields the peaceable **fruit of righteousness** to those who are exercised by it."*

As we continue our journey and quest to know Him, we will now encounter Him as The Truth; the One who sanctifies us and makes us ready to be used for His divine service. We are now ready to enter the Holy Place!

CHAPTER 5

PETITION-BASED PRAYER
(ASKING)

Communication is the most practical way of developing intimacy with anyone, including God. Prayer, therefore, is the most powerful tool we have as Christians to develop and maintain intimacy with God. In our progressive approach toward developing intimacy with God, it is necessary to discuss the three levels of prayer associated with the three areas of the Tabernacle. The three levels of prayer are *petition-based prayer, power-based prayer*, and *presence-based prayer*. These three levels also correspond to the three types of prayer Jesus described in His discourse with His disciples in Matthew Chapter 7, which are namely asking, seeking, and knocking.

In the following sections we will further explain the different levels of prayer associated with each area of the Tabernacle.

In the Outer Court we engage in the first level of prayer; what I call petition or need-based prayer. In this type of prayer, the needs of the believer are his or her primary focus in their relationship with God. This should not necessarily be surprising, given the fact that in the Outer Court the believer encounters Jesus as Savior, becomes born again, and thus begins his or her journey of intimacy with God. As a newborn baby, therefore, all he or she really cares for is daily provision and protection. As previously discussed, the level of maturity highlighted in the Outer Court is that of **little children**.

God our Father does not mind us talking to Him about our immediate and personal needs. In fact, He encourages it, and is willing and more than able to meet our needs. There is a plethora of scriptures that confirm this assessment and attitude of the Father, but we will only highlight a couple:

Matthew 7:7 – 10
"Ask, and it will be given to you; seek, and you will find; knock, and it will be opened to you. For everyone who asks receives, and the one who seeks finds, and to the one who knocks it will be opened. Or which one of you, if his son asks him for bread, will give him a

stone? Or if he asks for a fish, will give him a serpent? If you then, who are evil, know how to give good gifts to your children, how much more will your Father who is in heaven give good things to those who ask him! "

Philippians. 4:6:
"Do not be anxious about anything, but in everything by prayer and supplication with thanksgiving let your requests be made known to God..."

As these scriptures suggest, our Heavenly Father expects His children to be bold about coming to Him concerning their everyday needs. In fact, in the prayer that Jesus taught His disciples to pray, He made sure He included the part that has to do with the everyday needs of the believer; *"...Give us this day our daily bread..."* (**Matthew 6:11**).

The unfortunate thing is that many believers remain at this level of prayer for the majority of their Christian journey. They never really advance in their dialogue with God beyond focusing solely on their individual and material needs.

The sad fact is that most in the church today are just like the children of Israel after they were delivered from Egyptian bondage. Even though God had amazing things to show them about Himself, and to do through them to demonstrate His awesome power; they were more focused on their immediate material needs. The children of Israel were more interested in what God would give them, than what He could do through them. They could care less about what God's real agenda was in choosing them to be His peculiar people. God had already revealed to them that they were destined to become kings and priests in order to display His glory to the ends of the earth. However, all they really wanted was what they could eat and drink, and protection from their enemies. Of course, God was willing to oblige them and did supply their every need. He provided manna daily from heaven for forty years, and meat for every family enough to last several months. They were so well taken care of, that the shoes on their feet and the clothes on their back did not wear out for forty years. These redeemed slaves had every need met without their own sweat and toil. That is how good their God was to them!

Deuteronomy 29:5:
"I have led you forty years in the wilderness. Your clothes have not worn out on you, and your sandals have not worn off your feet."

God's plan for meeting all their needs, however, was for a greater purpose. By witnessing His power of providence and protection, they would be willing to proceed to their higher calling of establishing His Kingdom here on earth.

Deuteronomy 8:7 – 18:
"For the LORD your God is bringing you into a good land, a land of brooks of water, of fountains and springs, flowing out in the valleys and hills, a land of wheat and barley, of vines and fig trees and

*pomegranates, a land of olive trees and honey, a land in which you will eat bread without scarcity, in which you will lack nothing ... And you shall eat and be full, and you shall bless the LORD your God for the good land he has given you. "Take care lest you forget the LORD your God by not keeping his commandments and his rules and his statutes, which I command you today, lest, when you have eaten and are full and have built good houses and live in them, and when your herds and flocks multiply and your silver and gold is multiplied and all that you have is multiplied, then your heart be lifted up, and you forget the LORD your God, who brought you out of the land of Egypt, ... who led you through the great and terrifying wilderness, with its fiery serpents and scorpions and thirsty ground where there was no water, who brought you water out of the flinty rock, who fed you in the wilderness with manna that your fathers did not know, that he might humble you and test you, to do you good in the end. Beware lest you say in your heart, 'My power and the might of my hand have gotten me this wealth.' You shall remember the LORD your God, for it is he who gives you power to get wealth that **he may confirm his covenant** that he swore to your fathers, as it is this day."*

Like Israel of old, many in the kingdom today have consciously or unconsciously chosen to remain in their Outer Court experience with God. They are like children whose main focus is their own selfish needs. Most of their prayer time with God, individually or corporately, is focused on getting God to meet their personal needs. They fail to realize that there is so much more the Lord would love to talk with them about, including His desire to see His Kingdom manifested in their city and throughout the nations of the world. They have not yet learned to progress from the Outer Court to the Holy Place; from being children to young men; and from asking to seeking.

If you find yourself stuck in this place of complacency in prayer where most of your dialogue with the Father is based on your personal needs - provision, protection, comfort, and health, I admonish you to pause right now. I want you to ask the Lord to forgive you for focusing more on His hands - what He can give you, and not on His Heart - what He desires to do through you. Ask for grace to move on to the next level of prayer - which is seeking, or as I call it power-based prayer. We will discuss this in the next Section. Until then, meditate and act on this wonderful verse of scripture:

Psalms 27:8:
"You have said, "Seek my face." My heart says to you, "Your face, LORD, do I seek."

CHAPTER 6

THANKSGIVING

Our journey of intimacy with God also corresponds with our attitude of gratitude as we encounter God in each area of the Tabernacle. King David, also known as the sweet Psalmist of Israel, confirms this in Psalm 100:

Psalm 100:4:
*"Enter into His gates with **thanksgiving**, and into His courts with **praise**; be thankful to Him and **bless** His name."*

According to this passage, we begin our journey of intimacy with an attitude of thanksgiving in the Outer Court; then praise in the Holy Place; and then finally conclude with worship in the Holy of Holies. As we will further discuss, these attitudes of gratitude directly correspond with the three levels of prayer associated with each area of the Tabernacle.

The Psalmist said, *"enter His gates with thanksgiving..."* (Psalms 100:4a). The gates here represent the Outer Court of the Tabernacle where - as we have learned, we encounter Jesus as the Way, and are saved or justified by His blood.

An attitude of thanksgiving becomes our initial response to such a great salvation that we have experienced. When we recognize that we have been redeemed from sin to righteousness, from darkness to light, and from death to life; we cannot help but to be thankful!

This attitude of thankfulness is also a response to the graciousness of our Father for meeting our needs as His children in the Outer Court. As we have discussed in the previous chapter, the level of dialogue with the Father that is prevalent in the Outer Court is *petition-based prayer*. This type of prayer is mostly motivated by our natural needs - be it physical, emotional, or psychological etc. When the Lord satisfies these needs - as a true loving and caring Father, we respond with thanksgiving.

Let us furthermore remember that the only illumination in the Outer Court was provided by natural sun light. This means those who abide in the Outer Court of their relationship with the Lord, are only stimulated and motivated by their natural senses. These individuals are therefore thankful for what God does for them based solely on what they can see or feel, and not necessarily for who God is. Knowing who God is cannot be discerned by our natural senses but must be discerned by our spiritual senses.

Never-the-less, this attitude of gratitude is an important response that we need to have in our daily lives, as Paul stated many times in his Epistles, like Philippians 4:6.

Philippians 4:6:
*"Be careful for nothing; but in everything by prayer and supplication **with thanksgiving** let your requests be made known unto God..."*

As much as this attitude is appropriate and necessary, however, the Psalmist makes it clear that thanksgiving is just the beginning of our journey. This is our initial encounter with God through His Son Jesus, and what we do in the Outer Court. There is so much more that we have yet to experience as we press in to know Him further. As we advance into the Inner Court of the Tabernacle, we enter with Praise.

Psalms 100:4:
*"Enter into his gates with thanksgiving; and **into his courts with praise**..."*

We will discuss this level of gratitude in the next Section. In the meantime, take a moment right now and give the Lord thanks for all you know He has done for you. Like the song writer wrote:

"Count your blessings and name them one by one. Count your blessings and see what God has done. Count your blessings, name them one by one and you will see what the Lord has done".
~ (Song by JR Hutson and Johnson Oatman) Jr.)

SECTION TWO

JESUS, THE TRUTH
JESUS, MY SANCTIFIER
JESUS, OUR SANCTIFICATION

CHAPTER 7

THE HOLY PLACE

As stated in, Section 1, Chapter 2, before you and I advance into the Holy Place from the Outer Court, we must first encounter the *Brazen Laver*. This was simply a wash basin made of mirrors of brass and filled with water. It was placed between the brazen altar and the door to the Holy Place. It was here that the Priests would wash themselves from the blood stains of the sacrifices made on the altar before entering the Holy Place. It is significant to notice that the walls of the basin were made with mirrors which allowed the priests to see themselves clearly as they washed their hands and clothes with the water. They were thus cleansed thoroughly and -made spotless as they entered their next phase of service in the Holy Place. This clearly speaks of the power, essence, and the purpose of the Word of God in the life of the believer, as we will soon explain.

As we continue our journey of intimacy from the brazen altar to the Holy Place, we are suddenly reminded that we have been made Priests of the Most-High to make acceptable sacrifices unto Him.

1 Peter 2:5:
*"you also, as living stones, are being built up a spiritual house, **a holy priesthood**, to offer up spiritual sacrifices acceptable to God through Jesus Christ."*

I believe with all my heart that the priesthood of the believer is one of the greatest doctrines in the bible. However, it is also one of the least understood and emphasized in the church today by both clergy and laity alike. I also believe that before Jesus returns there is going to be a resurgence of teaching about the priesthood of the believer in its proper context as it relates to our intimacy with God, and His ultimate purpose for the believer. Even though this subject is being mentioned in this book, I intend to pen a more detailed description of the believer's role as a priest in another volume.

As we continue to focus our attention on the Inner Court of Moses' Tabernacle beginning with the Holy Place, we are drawn to the various elements beautifully and carefully arrayed on each side of the Tent of Meeting. On your right you will find the *Table of Showbread* made with acacia wood and overlaid with pure gold. On this table were placed twelve pieces of bread which were baked daily.

Exodus 25:23 – 30:

"You shall also make a table of acacia wood; two cubits shall be its length, a cubit its width, and a cubit and a half its height. And you shall overlay it with pure gold, and make a molding of gold all around... And you shall set the showbread on the table before Me always."

On the direct opposite side of the Table of Showbread was the *Golden Candlestick* or *Menorah*, as it is referred to by the Jews. This was a candlestick made of pure gold with six branches, with three on each side of the stem. This is very important to note as we shall soon discover.

Exodus 25:31 – 37:

""You shall also make a lampstand of pure gold; the lampstand shall be of hammered work. Its shaft, its branches, its bowls, its ornamental knobs, and flowers shall be of one piece. And six branches shall come out of its sides: three branches of the lampstand out of one side, and three branches of the lampstand out of the other side...You shall make seven lamps for it, and they shall arrange its lamps so that they give light in front of it."

What is the significance of the Holy Place and the elements represented there? What has that got to do with Jesus as the Truth? How does that impact our journey into intimacy with God? These are some of the questions we are going to answer as we proceed further in our journey of intimacy with the Lord.

The Holy Place represents a place of sanctification through the activity of the Word of God and the Spirit of God. Just as in the Outer Court we encounter Jesus as the Way, we encounter Him as the Truth in the Holy Place. In the Outer Court He becomes our Savior, and in the Holy Place He becomes our Sanctifier. As mentioned above, all the articles and elements in the Holy Place symbolize the activity of the Word and the Spirit of God bringing the believer into sanctification and service unto Him. Jesus described the activity of the Word of God and how we as believers can become cleansed and sanctified through it.

John 17:14 – 19:
"I have given them Your Word, and the world has hated them because they are not of the world, even as I am not of the world. I do not pray for You to take them out of the world, but for You to keep them from the evil. They are not of the world, even as I am not of the world. **Sanctify them through Your truth. Your Word is truth.** *As You have sent Me into the world, even so I have sent them into the world. And I sanctify Myself for their sakes, so that they also might be sanctified in truth."*

John 15:3:
"Now you are clean through the Word which I have spoken to you."

Let us take a moment to discuss the meaning of each piece of furniture and all the elements - components, furnishings, objects, found in the Holy Place.

The Brazen Laver

After the priests were done with the blood sacrifice, they would first wash themselves in the brazen laver before venturing into the Holy Place for service unto God on behalf of the people. This signified a cleansing of themselves from the filth of the people's sin represented by the sacrificial animal. The Apostle Paul reminds us that the way Jesus cleanses and sanctifies us as the Church His Bride is through the Word.

Ephesians 5:26 – 27:
*"that he might sanctify her, having cleansed her by the **washing of water with the word**, so that he might present the church to himself in splendor, without spot or wrinkle or any such thing, that she might be holy and without blemish."*

We also take note that the brazen laver was made like mirrors to reflect the image of the priest using it for the ceremonial washing. This is significant because James, the brother of Jesus, also reminds us that the Word of God is just like a mirror. It helps us to see who we are in Christ Jesus, while also helping us to identify the areas of our life that require adjustments.

James 1:22 – 24:
"But be doers of the word, and not hearers only, deceiving yourselves. For if anyone is a hearer of the

word and not a doer, he is like a man who looks intently at his natural face in a **mirror**. *For he looks at himself and goes away and at once forgets what he was like"*

The Table of Showbread

The Table of Showbread, which was to be replenished daily with fresh bread in the presence of God, represents the importance of fellowshipping daily in the Word of God for nourishment, strength, and sustainability.

Bread, as a symbol in the bible, always represents God's Word to His people. Just as bread is important for the daily sustenance of our physical bodies, because of its rich nutritional value; so also, is the Word of God important for our daily spiritual nourishment. God made this comparison to the children of Israel when He admonished them to not only depend on the natural bread, He provided for them daily in the wilderness - which they called "manna", but rather seek to be filled with the spiritual bread of the Word of God. Jesus also referenced this same scripture when He was tempted by Satan in the wilderness to turn a stone into bread in order to alleviate His physical hunger.

Deuteronomy 8:3:
"So, He humbled you, allowed you to hunger, and fed you with manna which you did not know nor did your fathers know, that He might make you know that **man shall not live by bread alone; but man lives by every word that proceeds from the mouth of the LORD."**

Luke 4:3 & 4:

"And the devil said to Him, "If You are the Son of God, command this stone to become bread." But Jesus answered him, saying, "It is written, 'man shall not live by bread alone, but by every word of God."

The Table of Showbread in the Holy Place therefore served as a reminder to the priests and the people about the importance of keeping the word of God as a priority in their daily lives. As priests of the Most-High God, and those who have been redeemed by the blood of Jesus to offer spiritual sacrifices unto God, we should be the primary examples as it relates to this. We need to keep the infallible Word of God before us daily if we are going to continue encountering our risen Savior as He leads us into intimacy with the Father.

It is also very significant that the Table of Showbread had to always contain twelve loaves of bread, which represented the twelve tribes of Israel. In other words, each tribe had to have its own loaf of bread represented in the presence of God. This means that God was interested in the personal devotion of each individual tribe, and not just the corporate devotion of the whole nation. If we are going to grow in intimacy and maturity as the Bride of Christ, then we need to return to our personal daily devotion in the Word of God, and not just depend on the weekly corporate word we receive from our spiritual leaders.

Another reason why God also compares His word with bread is that bread is the staple diet in almost every society today, just as it was in the days of Moses. In fact, bread is one of the most common, and essential commodities in the nutrition of mankind. Both rich and poor alike rely on bread for their daily nourishment because it is easily accessible to both. Likewise, the word of God is essential to our growth and spiritual nourishment, and is easily accessible, regardless of our socio-economic status. When you read, study, and apply the word of God daily, you will see your life blossom in intimacy with God as your bridegroom.

The Golden Candlestick

Unlike the Outer Court, where the primary source of illumination was natural sunlight, the main source of illumination in the Holy Place came from the Golden Candlestick. The priests were responsible to constantly tend to this light to ensure it was always burning to illuminate the Holy Place. The candlestick in the Holy Place represents the work that the Holy Spirit does to bring illumination of God's word to the believer. This produces sanctification and empowers the believer in his or her service to God.

It is important to understand that the reason why God asked Moses to fashion the candlestick the way he did was because He wanted us as believers to have a good perspective of who the Holy Spirit is in our lives, and how He leads us into fellowship and intimacy with the Father.

As already noted, the candlestick was constructed such that it had one main stem in the center out of which three branches extended on each side **(See Exodus 25:31 – 37)**. This gave it the appearance of having seven individual candlesticks that were all connected to one source. This structure illustrates perfectly who the Holy Spirit is in our lives. He is one Spirit but has seven main attributes or expressions which are all very important for the believer to develop intimacy with God.

John the Revelator was given the unique privilege and assignment to reveal this truth concerning the nature of the Trinity – the Father, Son, and Holy Spirit. He was taken up to Heaven and encountered all three personalities of the Trinity. In his awesome vision of the throne room, John witnessed not just the One who sat on the throne, but also encountered the Holy Spirit in all His glory and manifestations.

Revelation 4:4 & 5:
"Around the throne were twenty-four thrones, and on the thrones I saw twenty-four elders sitting, clothed in white robes; and they had crowns of gold on their heads. And from the throne proceeded Lightnings, thunderings, and voices. ***Seven lamps of fire were burning before the throne, which are the seven Spirits of God.*** *"*

John saw what God showed Moses on the mountain, which ultimately became the basic architecture of the Tabernacle. The seven lamps of fire burning before the throne in John's vision are the same as the Golden Candlestick in the Tabernacle of Moses. John also explains that these lamps of fire represent the seven Spirits of God.

What are the seven Spirits of God? Is John implying there are seven different Holy Spirits? Obviously not! To understand or explain this unique dilemma, it is important to reiterate that the Golden Candlestick had ONE central stem. Out of this stem, three branches extended on each side. This formed a total of seven individual branches, each having a candle. If we connect this to John's vision, we can safely conclude that what John saw was the Holy Spirit's seven illuminating attributes, which the Old Testament Prophet Isaiah also revealed.

In the Book of Isaiah chapter 11, this major prophet gives us insight into the seven expressions of the Holy Spirit. These expressions directly correspond to the seven branches of the Candlestick in Moses' Tabernacle, and to the "seven Spirits" in John's vision in the Book of Revelation.

Isaiah 11:2:
"The Spirit of the LORD shall rest upon Him, The Spirit of wisdom and understanding, The Spirit of counsel and might, The Spirit of knowledge and of the fear of the LORD."

In this scripture the central stem of the Candlestick is *"The Spirit"*. The scripture then highlights the six attributes of the Holy Spirit namely - *wisdom, understanding, counsel, might, knowledge, and the fear of the Lord.* According to this prophecy by Isaiah, the Messiah Jesus will be filled and empowered by the Holy Spirit with all His attributes fully expressed through Him in His earthly ministry. The good news is that this same Holy Spirit, with all His attributes, that rested on Jesus is now available to the believer who is now consciously trying to know Jesus more intimately as the Truth in the Holy Place, after encountering Him as the Way in the Outer Court. When you as a believer purpose to submit yourself to the sanctification process through God's word and are not controlled by your natural senses, then the Holy Spirit will also manifest Himself, with all these six attributes, to you and through you. This will continue to bring illumination, guidance, and direction; and will also ultimately empower you to live a life of adventure, victory, and service to God.

As you can see, four out of the six attributes associated with the Holy Spirit – *knowledge, wisdom, understanding, and counsel* - have a direct connection to His ability to lead and guide the believer into the truth of God's word. This tells us, as many scriptures also confirm, that the most important assignment of the Holy Spirit in the life of the believer is to bring him or her into the revelation of the knowledge of God:

1. Jesus described the Holy Spirit's assignment as One who will lead and guide the believer into all truth. *(See John 16:13 – 14)*
2. Paul the Apostle stated that the Holy Spirit is

here so that the believer will *know* what has been freely given to him. *(See 1 Cor. 2:9 – 12)*

3. Paul prayed for the Church in Ephesus that they would receive the *"Spirit of wisdom and revelation"* in the knowledge of God so that they (we) might *know* the *"hope of [their] calling..."* *(See Ephesians 1:17 – 19)*

These are only a few scriptures concerning the Holy Spirit's primary assignment to bring enlightenment to the believer through the Word of God. As we press in to know the Father more and more intimately, we are also introduced to the Holy Spirit's secondary role – which is to empower the believer for divine service as a priest. This role will be discussed momentarily.

Jesus My Sanctifier

When Jesus says He is the Truth, He is saying He is also the Sanctifier. What He uses to sanctify the believer is His word. He declared this in His High Priestly prayer for the Church before His death, burial, and resurrection. He asked the Father to sanctify His people with the truth of the word of God:

John 17:17:
*"Sanctify them by Your truth. **Your word is truth.**"*

John 15:3:
"You are already clean because of the word which I have spoken to you."

It is important to note that Jesus is the fulfillment of every element we see in the Tabernacle. Firstly, He is the Table of Showbread. He confirmed this many times when He described Himself as the "bread of life" and also as the "Word of God":

John 6:35:
"And Jesus said to them, "I am the bread of life. He who comes to Me shall never hunger..."

John 1:1 & 14:
"In the beginning was the Word, and the Word was with God, and the Word was God... And the Word became flesh and dwelt among us, and we beheld His glory, the glory as of the only begotten of the Father, full of grace and truth."

Secondly, Jesus also fulfilled the characteristics of the Golden Candlestick. In Isaiah 11:2, Isaiah prophetically describes the Holy Spirit's attributes from the context of who Jesus is, and what He was going to do.

Jesus was the first Man to exhibit the fullness of the Holy Spirit upon Him. According to the Gospel of John, Jesus received the Holy Spirit *without measure* as He submitted Himself to the Father in order to fulfill His assignment.

John 3:34:
"For He Whom God has sent speaks the Words of God, for God does not give the Spirit by measure."

Jesus set the example of what we as believers should expect to be and do, if we also submit to the Father and follow the leading of the Holy Spirit. It is no wonder Jesus taught His disciples extensively about the functions of the Holy Spirit, who would later come to dwell both within and upon them after His resurrection and ascension. The disciples needed to understand the importance of trusting and relying on the Holy Spirit, in order to guide them into all truth, and also empower them to fulfill the Great Commission. It is very important for us to acknowledge that we cannot know God and fulfill our destinies without a conscious relationship with the Holy Spirit who He has given to us as a gift to lead, guide, and empower us.

John 16:13 – 15:
"However, when He, the Spirit of truth, has come, He will guide you into all truth; for He will not speak on His own authority, but whatever He hears He will speak; and He will tell you things to come. He will glorify Me, for He will take of what is Mine and declare it to you. All things that the Father has are Mine. Therefore, I said that He will take of Mine and declare it to you".

Acts 1:8:
"But you will receive power when the Holy Spirit has come upon you, and you will be my witnesses in Jerusalem and in all Judea and Samaria, and to the end of the earth."

It is essential for the Body of Christ to revisit the doctrine of the Baptism in the Holy Spirit. Jesus is the One who baptizes us in the Holy Spirit. The baptism (*infilling*) of the Holy Spirit is a must for all who truly seek a vibrant and enduring love relationship with the Lord, and who also want to be empowered for service in the kingdom of God.

Luke 3:16:

"John answered, saying to all, "I indeed baptize you with water; but One mightier than I is coming, whose sandal strap I am not worthy to loose. He will baptize you with the Holy Spirit and fire."

If you have not already been baptized in the Holy Spirit, I encourage you to desire and ask the Lord to baptize you today. Although He is more than willing to fill you, He still desires that you seek Him first for this experience. Why don't you pause and pray this simple prayer with me right now?

*Dear Lord, I thank you that you have forgiven and saved me from my sins through your sacrifice on the cross of Calvary. Now, as a born-again son/daughter of yours, I ask you to baptize me in the Holy Spirit as You have promised to all those who ask and believe according to **Luke 11:13; John 7:37 – 39**. I receive the baptism of the Holy Spirit with the evidence of speaking in new tongues. Thank You Lord Jesus. Amen!*

If you prayed this prayer sincerely and in faith, I want you to know that Jesus answered you and just baptized you with the Holy Spirit. As proof of this baptism, the initial evidence you can expect to receive is your new prayer language which is speaking in new tongues. In addition, you will also receive a greater desire and understanding of the word of God. Take time to allow the Holy Spirit to accomplish His wonderful assignment in you as you draw closer to Him every day. He will make you a witness of who Jesus is. Hallelujah!

I believe Psalm 119 gives us the most succinct and in-depth analysis of the importance of the word of God in the believer's life. It highlights the power of God's word to sanctify, cleanse, and keep us from the lures of sin.

Psalms 119:9, 11, & 105:

"How can a young man cleanse his way? By taking heed according to your word... Your word I have hidden in my heart, that I might not sin against You...Your Word is a lamp to my feet, and a light to my path."

As you proceed to engage God in prayer with the help of the Holy Spirit, I encourage you to take some quality time to read, meditate, and pray Psalm 119 in its entirety. Allow these truths to be realized in your life. You will not be the same!

CHAPTER 8

YOUNG MEN

In our natural lives of human development, we grow from little children to young men/women, then into full grown adults. Just like in the natural, the spiritual life of a believer also matures from little children to young men/women, then ultimately adulthood. Unlike natural growth, however, spiritual maturity has little or nothing to do with the years of one's age. Rather develops out of a continual process from a lifestyle of intimacy with God. For example, there may be fifty-year-old men or women who have been saved for twenty or more years, but are still considered little children or immature, based on their lack of personal spiritual growth. On the contrary, there may be twenty-five or thirty-year old's who have only been saved for five years, but are considered young men/women, or even spiritually mature fathers/mothers.

One of Paul's frustrations in ministry was concerning the spiritual immaturity of the saints, whom he expected to be much further along in their spiritual growth and development than they were currently demonstrating.

1 Corinthians 3:1 – 2:
"And I, brethren, could not speak to you as to spiritual people but as to carnal, as to babes in Christ. I fed you with milk and not with solid food; for until now you were not able to receive it, and even now you are still not able."

In one of his most scathing indictments of the church, Paul addressed the immaturity of Christian believers in the book of Hebrews:

Hebrews 5:12 – 14:
*"For though by this time you ought to be teachers [mature], you need someone to teach you again the first principles of the oracles of God; and you have come to need milk and not solid food. For everyone who partakes only of milk is unskilled in the word of righteousness, for **he is a babe**. But solid food belongs to those who are of **full age**, that is, those who by reason of use have their senses exercised to discern both good and evil."*

As discussed in Chapter 2 (Section 1), those who encountered Jesus as the Way in the Outer Court were considered **little children** by the Apostle John. Paul admonishes Christians not to remain in this state, but to grow up and mature in their relationship with the Lord. In fact, according to Paul, one of the main reasons Jesus gave the church what we call "The Five-Fold Ministry" gifts of apostle, prophet, evangelist, pastor, and teacher, was to help equip the church as a whole, and to especially encourage members of the Body of Christ to grow into spiritual maturity.

Ephesians 4:11 – 14 (ESV):
*And he gave the apostles, the prophets, the evangelists, the shepherds, and teachers, to equip the saints for the work of ministry, for building up the body of Christ, until we all attain to the unity of the faith and of the knowledge of the Son of God, **to mature manhood**, to the measure of the stature of the fullness of Christ, **so that we may no longer be children...** Rather, speaking the truth in love**, we are to grow up** in every way into him who is the head, into Christ, ... when each part is working properly, **makes the body grow** so that it builds itself up in love.*

Unfortunately, in my estimation, the Body of Christ in many quarters have not been challenged and equipped enough by its leaders to mature into spiritual manhood. This is evidenced by the many divisions we still know exist in the Church, especially across denominational lines. However, I do believe that there is hope. I believe in these last days we are going to witness a maturing of the bride of Christ who will be equipped and ready to meet her Bridegroom as He descends from the clouds of heaven to rule in His eternal kingdom.

Just as the first stage of growth occurs in the Outer Court, the next phase of spiritual maturity and development occurs in the Holy Place, where we are all recognized as young men:

1 John 2:13 – 14:

"... I write to you, young men, because you have overcome the wicked one... I have written to you, young men, because you are strong, and the word of God abides in you, and you have overcome the wicked one."

As we can ascertain by this scripture, the main element that allows a person to be considered as a young man is the fact that *"...the word of God abides in you"*. The area of the Tabernacle with the most focus on the Word of God is the Holy Place, where the priests are sanctified and separated unto God for service. According to the Apostle John, the three characteristics which qualifies the believer to develop and mature from a ***little child*** into a young man are:

1. You are strong.
2. You have the word abiding in you.
3. You have overcome the wicked one.

It is important to note that all three of these qualities are directly linked to the activity of the Word and the Spirit of God in the life of the believer. As you progress in intimacy with the Lord and move past the

Outer Court into the Holy Place, you will be empowered by both the word of God and the Holy Spirit to live a life of sanctification and service to God. The Apostle Paul admonished believers through his letter to the church in Ephesus to *"be strong in the Lord"*:

Eph. 6:10:
*"Finally, my brothers, **be strong in the Lord** and in the power of His might."*

As Christians, instead of relying on our own strength or willpower to overcome the wicked one and his enticements to sin, we should rely rather on the ability of the Holy Spirit to strengthen and empower us to victory.

Zechariah 4:6:
"Then he answered and spoke to me, saying, this is the Word of Jehovah to Zerubbabel, saying, not by might, nor by power, but by My Spirit, says Jehovah of Hosts."

As previously described, one of the attributes of the Holy Spirit - as expressed by the candlestick in the Holy Place, is *might*. When a believer yields him or herself to the process of intimacy, I believe the *might* of the Holy Spirit will be demonstrated in two vital ways in their lives. The first is internally, or inwardly. In other words, the Holy Spirit supplies believers with strength in the inner-man and empowers him or her to live a victorious life worthy and pleasing to God.

Ephesians 3:16:
*"...that He would grant you, according to the riches of His glory, **to be strengthened with might by His Spirit in the inner man.**"*

Colossians 1:9 – 11:
*"For this cause we also, since the day we heard, do not cease to pray for you, and to desire that you might be filled with the knowledge of His will in all wisdom and spiritual understanding, that you might walk worthy of the Lord to all pleasing, being fruitful in every work and increasing in the knowledge of God, **being empowered with all power, according to the might of His glory**, to all patience and long-suffering with joyfulness..."*

As these scriptures confirm, the indwelling presence of the Holy Spirit within the child of God enables him or her to have the power to live right. Paul consciously and consistently prayed for his converts to be filled with the Holy Spirit, so that they would be empowered to fulfill their divine calling and destiny. This power, however, would remain dormant in their lives if they chose to stay in the Outer Court as little children, and allowed their natural senses to dominate their lives. The result is that they would be rendered fruitless and ineffective in their walk with God. You and I must yield to the inward promptings of the Holy Spirit so that we can produce the kind of fruit that is pleasing unto the Lord.

The second way the "*might*" of the Holy Ghost works for the believer to develop into a ***young man*** is externally, or outwardly. In this instance, the Holy Spirit strengthens and empowers the believer to become an effective witness as a minister of the gospel. Before His ascension to heaven, Jesus made it clear to His disciples that the Holy Spirit's power would be required to restore God's original purpose for man through the Great Commission.

Luke 24:49:
*"And behold, I send the promise of My father on you. But you sit in the city of Jerusalem until you are **clothed with power** from on high."*

Acts 1:8:
*"But you shall **receive power**, after the Holy Spirit coming upon you. And you shall be witnesses to Me both in Jerusalem and in all Judea, and in Samaria, and to the end of the earth."*

It is unfortunate that there are some who have attempted to accomplish the Great Commission without the power of the Holy Spirit. There are others who also continue to minimize and even deny the importance of the Holy Spirit in Christian ministry today. They choose rather to rely on their own ability, acumen, and psychological prowess to accomplish anything for God. It is no wonder that it seems the Church in many parts of the world looks weak, powerless, and ineffective in the face of a demonically inspired agenda to keep a whole generation bound in sin and spiritual darkness.

Jesus was not playing games when He instructed His disciples to go tarry in Jerusalem until they were endued with Holy Ghost power from on high. He knew that salvation, healing, and deliverance from sin, sickness and spiritual darkness could only be accomplished by, and through the power and *might* of the Holy Spirit. After ten days of tarrying in the upper room in Jerusalem, these weak-kneed, unimpressive, and uneducated disciples, received the power of the Holy Ghost on the Day of Pentecost. Not only were they transformed into new people, but they also received the ability to completely transform their known world within a span of a century. The Book of Acts is the chronicle of the early church in action. We should always use the early church in the Book of Acts as the model and yardstick whereby we determine whether the 21st Century Church is in alignment with the Lord's original intention for His church.

I believe with all my heart that God intends for the Book of Acts to be our floor, not our ceiling, our starting point, and not our ending point. He expects us to surpass what the early church accomplished in one-hundred years through the power of the Holy Spirit. I believe we will do just that as we also *wait on* the Holy Spirit until we are endued with supernatural power to save the lost, heal the sick, deliver the bound, and raise the dead. We are quickly approaching the precipice of a Holy Ghost cultural awakening and spiritual revival that will make the Day of Pentecost pale in comparison. Whether you are in fulltime ministry or not, I strongly admonish you to be constantly filled with the Holy Spirit so that you too can be effectively used by God to bring transformation to the world around you.

Ephesians 5:18:

*"And do not get drunk with wine, for that is debauchery, **but be filled with the Spirit.**"*

CHAPTER 9

FRUIT OF MINISTRY

As we continue in the journey of intimacy with God through the Holy Place, we need to bear **more fruit**. We identified that the fruit produced in the Outer Court is the Fruit of Repentance, or the Fruit of Righteousness. The *more fruit* we need to produce in the Holy Place is the *Fruit of Ministry*.

As we have already discussed, the Holy Place was the area where the priests accomplished most of their duties. It was the place where dual ministry acts were practiced and perfected - ministry to God on behalf of the people, and ministry to the people on behalf of God. Since the Holy Place represents our encounter with Jesus as the Truth - the One who sanctifies us unto God and His service, we need to point out that the priests were also sanctified before performing their duties unto God and the people. In fact, if they did not follow the sanctification rituals ordained by God through Moses, they were automatically disqualified for service.

2 Chronicles 29:4 – 34:

"And he brought in the priests and the Levites and gathered them into the east street. And he said to them, Hear me, Levites, now **sanctify yourselves** *and sanctify the house of Jehovah, the God of your fathers, and carry out the filthiness out of the* **holy place**...*And they gathered their brothers and sanctified themselves, and came, according to the command of the king, by the words of Jehovah, to clean the house of Jehovah...But the priests were too few, so that they could not skin all the burnt offerings. And their brothers the Levites helped them until the work was ended, and* **until the priests had sanctified themselves**. *For the Levites were more upright of heart to make themselves pure than the priests"*

As we proceed in our journey in intimacy with the Father, we need to recognize and faithfully fulfill our duties as priests of the Most-High God so we can consistently produce fruit. The Lord expected this from His disciples once they learned to abide in His presence:

John 15:16:

"You did not choose me, but I chose you and appointed you that **you should go and bear fruit** *and that your fruit should abide, so that whatever you ask the Father in my name, he may give it to you."*

Being a faithful and fruitful servant or minister of the Lord should be one of the highest goals toward which all Christians should aim to achieve. I believe we will all like to hear our Lord on the Day od Judgement say to us, *"Well done good and faithful servant ..."* **(Matthew 25:21)**. The Word of God is replete with examples of what our *fruit of ministry* should look like. However, one example stands out from among the many. I believe the life of the Apostle Paul serves as a great example of the kind of fruitfulness in ministry toward which all of us should strive to attain. After his salvation encounter with the Lord on the road to Damascus, Paul used mighty signs and wonders to bear witness of the resurrection of the Lord Jesus Christ.

The fruit of Paul's ministry is evident by his Epistles. His life and ministry were so impactful that the Holy Spirit chose to use his letters as the foundation of church theology and doctrine. The Apostle Paul, however, will be the first to tell you that his success in ministry was not based on his intellectual prowess - which surpassed most of his contemporaries. His success was rather based on his desire to display the power of God everywhere he went. This desire was expressed in Paul's first letter to the Corinthian church. In his description of his initial ministry encounter with them, he states that he made a conscious decision before arriving in Corinth:

1 Corinthians 2:1 – 3:
"And I, brethren, when I came unto you, came not with excellency of speech or of wisdom, proclaiming to you the testimony of God. For I determined not to know

anything among you, save Jesus Christ, and him crucified ... And my speech and my preaching were not in persuasive words of wisdom, but in **demonstration of the Spirit and of power.**"

Why did Paul - a proven, established and well acclaimed religious scholar of his day according to his own biography in **Philippians 3:3 - 6**, decide not to rely on his intellectual genius when communicating the gospel to the Corinthians, but rather chose to depend upon the power of the Holy Ghost? He gives us the answer in the next verse:

"that your faith should not stand in the wisdom of men, but in the power of God" **(1 Corinthians 2:5)**

Paul concluded that for the gospel to have a long-lasting impact on the lives of his converts, it had to be delivered through the power of the Holy Spirit, and not through the wisdom or intellectual prowess of men. He realized that in order to fulfill the Lord's command to His disciples in John 15, he would have to stay intimately connected to the Vine. It is the life of the Vine that enables its branches to bear fruit that remains.

John 15:4, 5, 16:
"Abide in me, and I in you. As the branch cannot bear fruit of itself, except it abides in the vine; so neither can ye, except ye abide in me. I am the vine, ye are the branches: He that abides in me, and I in him, the same bears much fruit: for apart from me ye can do nothing...Ye did not choose me, but I chose you, and appointed you, that ye should go and bear fruit, and that your fruit should abide..."

Another intriguing question worth exploring is: why does Paul go out of his way to inform us that he made his decision not to rely on his excellency of speech when he came to the Corinthians? Wasn't this his "modus-operandi" from the very beginning of his ministry anyway? Surely it was, especially after he was commissioned as an Apostle to the Gentiles and sent on his first missionary journey from Antioch (*See Acts 13*). In fact, Acts Chapters 14 through 16 describe two missionary journeys that Paul, Barnabas, and their other companions undertook. In these chapters we see the gospel spread through Gentile territory like wildfire because of the mighty signs and wonders God wrought through these Apostles, despite the hostility they faced from Jews in this region.

There was no place in that territory that Paul and his team went that you do not see the kingdom of darkness being rattled at its core as the gospel was being preached and new churches were being established. Without a doubt, wherever Paul and his team went there was either a revival and/or a riot that took place. In other words, there was always a spiritual reaction that impacted the way the people responded to the Gospel in that region. Devout Jews and Gentiles alike were coming into the kingdom in droves, which really disturbed the socio-economic, political, and religious status-quo of that day and of that region. Once the people of God like Paul came to town, there was a shift in the atmosphere and the system of the world had to respond to the gospel. For example, when Paul and his team arrived in Thessalonica with their Holy Ghost action campaign, this was the response of the people: *"These men who have turned the world upside down have come here also..."* **(Acts 17:6)**

However, something changed in Paul's approach when he arrived in Athens later in Acts 17. While he waited for his team to join him from Thessalonica, he was grieved by what he observed in the city. It was a city given to so much idolatry, that one idol was dedicated to *"the unknown god"*. This moved him to engage the city's religious and intellectual elite in what is known as his "Mars Hill" sermon. This famous sermon has been hailed by Christian theologians and scholars as one of the most powerful sermons ever preached. It has also been presented to many bible college and seminary students as the model for sermon preparation and delivery[3].

I do not disagree that Paul's message to these Stoics and Epicureans - the philosophical elites of that day, was powerful, especially in its content, scope, and depth of theology. However, the result of his approach and delivery did not yield the kind of fruit that we have come to expect from Paul's ministry. There was neither revival nor any riots after he preached his message. The ears of the people were tickled alright, but the status-quo remained largely the same. The Bible describes the attitude of the people after they heard his sermon, and the results that followed:

Acts 17:32 – 34:
"Now when they heard of the resurrection of the dead, some mocked. But others said, "We will hear you again

about this." So, Paul went out from their midst. But some men joined him and believed, among whom also were Dionysius the Areopagite and a woman named Damaris and others with them."

The people's response must have disappointed Paul, to say the least. He had just preached the greatest sermon of his life, and yet unlike before, there was not a throng of converts following him, nor was he beaten, stoned, or cast away. There was a stalemate in the conflict between the kingdom of darkness and the kingdom of light over the souls and destinies of the people in that region. Paul understood this scenario well and knew that he had failed to plant the flag of the kingdom of God in that region. We should also know that whenever there is no clear winner in the on-going conflict between the kingdom of Satan and the kingdom of God over territories, Satan's kingdom will still have a dominant influence in that region. In other words, whenever the social, political, economic, and religious structures of any region are unaffected by the church, the kingdom of darkness still has sway, and it becomes more arduous for any long-lasting fruit of the gospel to be manifested in that region.

Paul had allowed himself to be influenced by his audience and surroundings unlike at any other previous time. I guess he thought if he could appeal to their philosophical and intellectual affinities, he would persuade them into the kingdom of God. No wonder he quoted some of their own poets in his sermon about their need for a Savior (**See Acts 17:28**). In this instance he relied more on the *wisdom of men* rather than the *power of God* to reach these unregenerate philosophers. This mistake resulted in the least impactful ministry encounter of his career. Although a few people were converted, there was no long-lasting fruit in that city. In fact, I do not recall it being mentioned anywhere that a strong church was established in Athens like most of the other cities he visited such as Galatia, Philippi, and Thessalonica, to name a few. This, my friend, is the backdrop for Paul's statement to the Corinthians which was previously referenced in 1 Corinthians 2:1-3.

The next city Paul found himself in after his colossal failure in Athens, was the city of Corinth about 65 miles away[4]. Although Corinth was very reminiscent of Athens and full of philosophers, it was also much more worldly and ungodly, being the cosmopolitan district of commerce in Asia Minor. I believe after reviewing his last campaign and thoroughly consulting the Lord in prayer, Paul made up his mind to never allow himself to be influenced by his audience or surroundings again. He decided to lay aside his intellectual brilliance and solely depend on the Holy Spirit to work through him in order to touch the people's hearts, rather than just their minds. He fully understood that it is only through the anointing of the Holy Spirit that fruit can be produced in us – that is fruit that will remain. Unsurprisingly, that was the result of the missionary campaign in Corinth. Once again Paul's evangelistic campaign resulted in both a revival and a riot, out of which many people were saved and delivered.

Acts 18:1, 8:

*"After this Paul left Athens and went to Corinth... Crispus, the ruler of the synagogue, believed in the Lord, together with his entire household. And **many of the Corinthians** hearing Paul believed and were baptized."*

It is imperative for us to understand that all these things were written as an example for us (**1 Corinthians 10:6**). If we are going to achieve the kind of fruit the Apostle Paul and many of our early church fathers experienced in both life and ministry, we need to follow their example and refuse to settle for preaching, teaching, evangelism, or even singing that is void of God's Holy Ghost power. Our goal should never be to just tickle the ears or intellect of our audience. We should never be satisfied when our ministries or churches do not disturb the status-quo in our communities, cities, and regions. Like Paul, we should always expect a revival because of our presence in the regions God has placed us in. The kingdom of darkness should never feel comfortable when the kingdom of light shows up. Paul sums up the fruit of his ministry in this way:

Romans 15:17 – 19:

*"In Christ Jesus, then, I have reason to be proud of my work for God. For I will not venture to speak of anything except what Christ has accomplished through me to bring the Gentiles to obedience—**by word and deed, by the power of signs and wonders, by the power of the Spirit of God**—so that from Jerusalem and all the way around to Illyricum I have fulfilled the ministry of the gospel of Christ."*

My dear friend, this is the kind of testimony I want. This is the type of fruit I want to bear because of my ministry. What about you?

Like Paul declares, this fruit can only come forth when we rely more on the power of the Holy Spirit, than on our own human, intellectual, or educational prowess. You can strive to obtain all the degrees you want, just remember that real fruit only comes from being intimately acquainted with the One who truly empowers us for Gospel ministry. It comes as a result of waiting on the Lord in prayer (and fasting) and following the leading of the Holy Spirit. Let us proceed therefore to talk about the kind of prayer that is required to generate fruit that abides forever and creates lasting impact.

CHAPTER 10

POWER-BASED PRAYER
(SEEKING)

After encountering Jesus as the Truth in the Holy Place, the next level of prayer for the believer who progresses past the brazen altar is what I call **power-based praying**. Jesus referred to this in Matthew 7:7 as **seeking**.

Matthew 7:7:
"Ask and it will be given to you; seek and you will find; knock and the door will be opened to you."

At this level of communication in intimacy with the Father, the believer is more focused on seeking the heart of the Father. In so doing, he positions himself to receive power to do ministry more effectively. Although his focus was on his personal needs in the Outer Court, now he can begin to appreciate his priestly calling much more as he submits himself to be sanctified by the word of God. He is no longer a *child* subject to his own carnal desires and disposition but is now considered a *young man* who is *"strong in the Lord and in the power of His might"* (**Ephesians 6:10**). He has also now embraced his calling to be a witness who understands the need for the power of the Holy Spirit to accomplish anything of significance for God and His Kingdom.

If we are not careful, however, this wonderful discovery can lead us to the place where we become so satisfied with just receiving God's power in ministry, that we completely miss out on experiencing His person and presence. You may be asking - aren't they the same thing, or is there really a difference between the two? Yes...there is a marked difference between God's power and His presence. You can experience God's power without His tangible presence in your life, but it is impossible to experience His presence and not have His power working through you. We will speak more about this in the final section of this book.

We should never be satisfied with just having the power of God in our lives or ministry. Let us always seek to go after the presence, and most importantly after the glory! Let us be like Moses who - after experiencing the power of God more than any other human, still asked the Lord to show him His glory.

Exodus 33:13 – 18:

*"Now therefore, if I have found favor in your sight, please show me now your ways, that I may know you in order to find favor in your sight. Consider too that this nation is your people." And he said, "My presence will go with you, and I will give you rest." And he said to him, "If your presence will not go with me, do not bring us up from here. For how shall it be known that I have found favor in your sight, I and your people? Is it not in your going with us, so that we are distinct, I and your people, from every other people on the face of the earth?" And the LORD said to Moses, "This very thing that you have spoken I will do, for you have found favor in my sight, and I know you by name." Moses said, **"Please show me your glory."***

In order for us to see God's power in both our lives and in the church in a greater dimension, it is important for us to renew our commitment to seeking His face again. We need to become like David, whose passionate desire was to encounter God's power afresh so that he could overcome his adversaries.

Psalms 63:1 – 2

*"A Psalm of David, when he was in the wilderness of Judah. O God, You are my God; **I shall seek You earnestly**; My soul thirsts for You, my flesh yearns for You, In a dry and weary land where there is no water. Thus I have seen You in the sanctuary, **To see Your power and Your glory***"

I believe this should also be our own personal desire and prayer. There is a tremendous need in the church today for the release of God's power again like it was displayed in the days of Moses, David, Elijah, and Paul. Miracles, signs, and wonders should once again become the norm, and not the exception. This is not only the will of the Father, but also a requirement. God never intended for the church to operate without the evidence of the resurrection of our Lord and Savior Jesus Christ. This is the reason why the Lord commanded the disciples to tarry in Jerusalem until they were *"endued with power from on high"*. Once the disciples were empowered by the Holy Spirit, then the Lord could commission them to go into all the world and make disciples. In the Book of Acts, the Lord made it clear that their assignment was to **become** witnesses unto Him. For this to happen, they had to receive the power of the Holy Spirit on the day of Pentecost. It is interesting today that instead of *being* witnesses for God, most people would rather settle for *doing* witnessing. Although passing out gospel tracts and knocking on a few doors to *witness* is good, it falls far below what the Master intended for His Church.

To *be* a *witness* in any court of law means you must provide evidence, or proof to corroborate the assertion of guilt or innocence for the party you represent, whether they are the plaintiff or defendant. In much the same way, we as *witnesses* of our Lord must produce evidence or proof to corroborate the fact that Jesus died, and rose again on the third day with resurrection power. He is currently alive and seated at the right hand of Majesty; and is getting ready to return once again to the earth with glory and power. The assignment Jesus gave His church was for born again believers to be *proof-producers5*. You are a proof-producer!

One of the greatest travesties that can ever happen to a prosecutor trying to put away a dangerous criminal, or a defense attorney trying to prove the innocence of a defendant is to have someone who claims to be a witness, show up with little or no evidence to corroborate the testimony of the party they represent. In much the same way it is a travesty when it seems the church is incapable of producing proof that Jesus is still alive and well. We need to prove that Jesus is still the same today as He was yesterday and will be tomorrow **(Hebrews 13:8)**. We need to provide evidence that He is still healing the sick, delivering those who are bound, raising the dead, and feeding the hungry soul.

As we discussed in the previous chapter, the Apostle Paul decided to always be a *proof-producer*, except when he fell into the trap of relying on his intellectual wisdom, instead of on the power of the Holy Spirit when he was in Athens. The Apostle Paul teaches us that the only way to be a *witness* and produce evidence of the resurrection is to allow the Holy Spirit to have His way in our lives by manifesting His power through signs and wonders.

In fact, the only way Jesus could also prove who He was while on earth, was through mighty signs and wonders God wrought through Him by the Holy Spirit. The Gospels are replete with assertions Jesus made to this fact. Let me reference the Apostle Peter, however, who was with Jesus from the beginning of His earthly ministry all the way up to His death, burial, resurrection, and ascension to heaven. How did God prove that Jesus was who He said He was? Listen to the Apostle Peter:

Acts 2:22:
*"Men of Israel, hear these words: Jesus of Nazareth, **a man attested to you by God with mighty works and wonders and signs** that God did through him in your midst, as you yourselves know."*

Just like Jesus, the only way we as born again, Holy Ghost filled children of God, are going to prove that we are who we say we are through the evidence of signs and wonders. Nothing less will suffice. Therefore, it is imperative for us to return to our *upper rooms* instead of our *supper rooms*; and to fasting and praying instead of feasting and playing. Waiting on the Lord again in prayer until we are endued with power from on high is not an option, but a requirement. More than ever before, this should be a vital necessity in our generation today.

If we are going to have the kind of results that Jesus and the early disciples had, especially the Apostle Paul, we must do what they did. Jesus, our ultimate example, and model spent days and nights in prayer (***See Mark 1:35***). The Apostle Paul was also himself a man given to consistent fasting and praying (***See 2 Cor. 11:27***). In fact, one of the greatest desires and prayers of Paul, which should become our own, is found in his epistle to the Philippians:

Philippians 3:10:

"That I may know him, and the power of his resurrection, and the fellowship of his sufferings, being made conformable to his death."

This scripture reveals Paul's main focus was to grow in his knowledge and intimacy with the Lord. Through that intimacy he was able to experience the power of Jesus' resurrection in order to become both an effective witness, and *proof-producer* of the resurrected King of kings and Lord of lords.

Let us get back into our prayer closets and begin a renewed cry for God to release His mighty power from on high. He wants to do it more than we desire it. It's time to move from *petition-based* prayers to *power-based* prayers, and from *asking* to *seeking*.

In our final section we will discuss an even more excellent way of prayer, the art of *knocking*, or what I call *presence-based* prayer. As you proceed, let me leave you with this scripture:

Hosea 10:12:

"Sow to yourselves in righteousness, reap in mercy; break up your fallow ground: for it is time to seek the LORD, till he come and rain righteousness on you."

CHAPTER 11

PRAISE

During our journey of intimacy with the Father, the attitude of gratitude displayed in the Holy Place is that of praise. The Psalmist gives us three levels of gratitude, which corresponds with the three areas of the Tabernacle. First, we enter His gates (Outer Court) with thanksgiving (Section I Chapter 5), then into His courts (Holy Place) with praise.

As we learned earlier, the only type of sanctioned activity allowed in the Holy Place is offered by those who have accepted their calling as sanctified priests of the Lord. It is important to note that the priest's primary function was to offer sacrifices on behalf of the people. God's original plan was for all His chosen people - first the Israelites, and subsequently the church to ultimately become priests and kings.

Exodus 19:5 – 6:

"Now therefore, if ye will obey my voice indeed, and keep my covenant, then ye shall be a peculiar treasure unto me above all people: for all the earth is mine: And ye shall be unto me a kingdom of priests, and an holy nation..."

1 Peter 2: 9:

"But ye are a chosen generation, a royal priesthood, an holy nation, a peculiar people; that ye should shew forth the praises of him who hath called you out of darkness into his marvelous light"

It is interesting that the Apostle Peter associates the purpose of our priesthood calling with *"showing forth the praises of Him..."*. As priests of the Lord this means our main assignment on earth is centered around bringing praise, glory, and honor to the One who called us, and anointed us to become priests (***See also Revelation 1:6***). As it relates to our journey into intimacy with God, however, this assignment cannot be achieved in the Outer Court. It must take place in the Holy Place, where the activities of the Spirit and the Word are enhanced in the Believer's life.

In the Book of Hebrews, the Apostle Paul introduces another dimension of our priestly duties that we should offer unto the Lord while ministering in the Holy Place – the sacrifice of praise!

Hebrews 13:10 – 15:

"We have an altar, whereof they have no right to eat which serve the tabernacle. For the bodies of those

beasts, whose blood is brought into the sanctuary by the high priest for sin, are burned without the camp. Wherefore Jesus also, that he might sanctify the people with his own blood, suffered without the gate. ...By him therefore let us offer the sacrifice of praise to God continually, that is, the fruit of our lips giving thanks to his name..."

You may be asking, what is the difference between this attitude of praise, and the attitude of thanksgiving described in Section I? We give thanks to God for what we can perceive He has done with our natural senses, whereas we praise Him for what we cannot yet perceive naturally that He has done but know by revelation knowledge. In other words, our thanksgiving in the Outer Court is based on facts, but our praise in the Holy Place is based on faith and truth. In the Outer Court, the main light that brings illumination to the believer is natural sunlight. In the Holy Place, however, illumination for the mature believer comes from the candlestick - which represents the seven attributes of the Holy Spirit.

Just as we grow in our prayer life from *asking* in the Outer Court to *seeking* in the Holy Place, we also need to advance from thanksgiving to praise. Likewise, as we thank God for what He gives us when we ask, we also need to praise Him for releasing His power in our lives to be His witnesses.

SECTION THREE

JESUS, THE LIFE
JESUS, MY SUPERIOR JOY
JESUS, OUR GLORIFICATION

CHAPTER 12

THE HOLY OF HOLIES

After experiencing Jesus as the Way in the Outer Court, and the Truth in the Holy Place; our journey into intimacy climaxes in the Holy of Holies - where we experience Jesus as the Life.

In every area of the Tabernacle Jesus plays a significant role in the believer's life and offers a different benefit of salvation. In the Outer Court He becomes our Savior, and we experience justification from our sins. In the Holy Place He becomes our Sanctifier, and we experience sanctification. Finally, in the Holy of Holies, Jesus becomes our superior joy, and we experience glorification. This last experience should be the apex of our Christian journey. Unfortunately, many go through their Christian lives and never attain this level of intimacy with the Lord.

The Most Holy Place, also known as the Holy of Holies, was the most sacred place on earth from the time of the Tabernacle of Moses, until the resurrection of our Lord Jesus Christ. This most holy part of the Tabernacle had a restricted and exclusive access to ONLY one person – the High Priest. Once a year on the "Day of Atonement", the High Priest was the only one granted access to take the blood of the lamb slain from the brazen altar in the Outer Court to the Holy of Holies. The High Priest would then sprinkle the blood on the "Mercy Seat" for the atonement of the sins of the nation.

Unlike the Outer Court and the Holy Place, there was only one piece of furniture in the Most Holy Place - the Ark of the Covenant. Since the Ark represented both the very throne and presence of God on earth, it could be considered the most important piece of furniture throughout all history.

Moses was instructed to build the Ark with delicate care according to the pattern of God's throne which was revealed to him on Mount Sinai. This same revelation was given to the prophet's Isaiah and Ezekiel, and most of all to the Apostle John in the Book of Revelation.

Exodus 25:10 – 22:
""And they shall make an ark of acacia wood; two and a half cubits shall be its length, a cubit and a half its width, and a cubit and a half its height. And you shall overlay it with pure gold, inside and out you shall overlay it, and shall make on it a molding of gold all

around. You shall cast four rings of gold for it, and put them in its four corners; two rings shall be on one side, and two rings on the other side... You shall put the poles into the rings on the sides of the ark, that the ark may be carried by them...And you shall put into the ark the Testimony which I will give you. "You shall make a mercy seat of pure gold; two and a half cubits shall be its length and a cubit and a half its width. And you shall make two cherubim of gold; of hammered work you shall make them at the two ends of the mercy seat. Make one cherub at one end, and the other cherub at the other end; you shall make the cherubim at the two ends of it of one piece with the mercy seat. And the cherubim shall stretch out their wings above, covering the mercy seat with their wings, and they shall face one another; the faces of the cherubim shall be toward the mercy seat. You shall put the mercy seat on top of the ark, and in the ark you shall put the Testimony that I will give you. And there I will meet with you, and I will speak with you from above the mercy seat, from between the two cherubim which are on the ark of the Testimony, about everything which I will give you in commandment to the children of Israel."

Isaiah 6:1 – 3:

"In the year that King Uzziah died, I saw the Lord sitting on a throne, high and lifted up, and the train of His robe filled the temple. Above it stood seraphim; each one had six wings: with two he covered his face, with two he covered his feet, and with two he flew. And one cried to another and said: "Holy, holy, holy is the LORD of hosts; The whole earth is full of His glory!""

Revelation 4:1 – 4:

"... Immediately I was in the Spirit; and behold, a throne set in heaven, and One sat on the throne. And He who sat there was like a jasper and a sardius stone in appearance; and there was a rainbow around the throne, in appearance like an emerald. Around the throne were twenty-four thrones, and on the thrones I saw twenty-four elders sitting, clothed in white robes; and they had crowns of gold on their heads" And from the throne proceeded lightnings, thunderings, and voices. Seven lamps of fire were burning before the throne, which are the seven Spirits of God. Before the throne there was a sea of glass, like crystal. And in the midst of the throne, and around the throne, were four living creatures full of eyes in front and in back."

As these scriptures describe, God wants His throne and all the activity surrounding it to be the center of attraction for His people here on earth, just as it appears in heaven. Without the Ark of the Covenant in the Most Holy Place, the Tabernacle was just another ordinary tent. The activities described in the other areas were also utterly meaningless and simply religious. Without the presence and glory of God being our primary focus, every church building is just that - a plain building. All our Christian activities and services will therefore also be rendered meaningless and just plain religious.

Consider this analogy - the airplane designated to transport the President of the United States to and from long destinations is known as Air Force One. It was a revelation to me when I discovered that even though there is a specific custom-made aircraft for this assignment, whatever plane the President boards automatically by default becomes Air Force One. In other words, it is the presence of the President aboard the plane that gives it significance and makes the difference, not just the plane by itself. Without the President's actual presence, it may pass as just another regular airplane.

Without the Ark of Covenant, the Tabernacle was just another tent filled with some expensive items. Without the presence of the Lord in our churches, they are just empty and insignificant monuments waiting to be dumped in the ash heap of history. Without the presence of Jesus in your life, you are just like the living-dead, a hopeless and restless soul!

Remember Shiloh!

This recalls one of the most infamous episodes in the history of the nation of Israel. After Joshua settled the people in the Promised Land, they were governed by Judges who were appointed by the LORD. Many of these Judges also served as Priests. As part of their priestly duties, the Judges were responsible for overseeing the Ark of the Covenant, which represented God's manifested presence among His chosen people. One such Judge was Eli the Priest - who together with his corrupt sons, ministered to the Lord and the people. It is important to note that the place where Eli and his sons lived and where the Ark was kept became the most popular, and prominent city throughout the land. This city was called Shiloh! The whole nation came to Shiloh for only one reason – to worship God and to bring their sacrifices before His presence. As long as the Ark of God was there, Shiloh was the place to be.

Everything, however, changed on that fateful day when the Philistines defeated Israel in battle and captured the Ark of God. The very life and essence of the city disappeared with the presence of God. More than anyone else, Eli fully understood the impact and devastation of losing the Ark. This meant God's manifested presence – the very life and essence of the city, had utterly disappeared and would no longer be with them. When Eli heard that the Ark had been captured by the enemy, he fell off his chair and broke his neck and died. Without the Ark of God in Shiloh, the city was now insignificant, and the people were left without any defense against their enemies.

1 Samuel 4:17 – 18:
"He who brought the news answered and said, "Israel has fled before the Philistines, and there has also been a great defeat among the people. Your two sons also, Hophni and Phinehas, are dead, and the ark of God has been captured." **As soon as he mentioned the ark of God,** *Eli fell over backward from his seat by the side of the gate, and his neck was broken and he died ..."*

Eli's daughter-in-law, while in the throes of childbirth, prophetically captured the reality of what transpired with her last dying breath by naming her newborn son "Ichabod", meaning *the glory has departed.* It was not the defeat of the Israelites in battle, or the death of her husband that triggered this response, but rather that the Glory and presence of Jehovah had departed not just from Shiloh, but also from Israel.

1 Samuel 4:19 – 22:
"Now his daughter-in-law, the wife of Phinehas, was pregnant, about to give birth. And when she heard the news that the ark of God was captured, and that her father-in-law and her husband were dead, she bowed and gave birth, for her pains came upon her. And about the time of her death the women attending her said to her, "Do not be afraid, for you have borne a son." But she did not answer or pay attention. And she named the child Ichabod, saying, "The glory has departed from Israel!" because the ark of God had been captured and because of her father-in-law and her husband. And she said, "The glory has departed from Israel, for the ark of God has been captured.""

The truth is, unlike many in the Body of Christ, the Israelites not only understood, but also put a high premium on the presence of God in their midst. Today in many churches across the globe, spiritual leaders and parishioners do not even recognize or care whether His presence is in their midst or not. I dare say that *Ichabod* is written over the door posts of a lot of these churches. Unfortunately, what is sad is that the people in those churches either do not know it, or they just do not care.

In my relatively brief time serving the Lord, I have observed how much effort many put in making the church building look beautiful, while on the contrary less effort is used to ensure that God's presence is manifest in their midst. I have witnessed firsthand my share of beautiful cathedrals with stained glass windows, padded pews, and crystal chandeliers, but none possessed an ounce of the Presence and Power of God in their midst. On the other hand, I have attended worship services in tents, classrooms, and even storefronts where God's glorious presence was tangibly manifested. It is time we pursue the presence of God over anything else because His presence is what truly makes the difference. Once again, let us remember Shiloh!

Remember Solomon's Temple!

God does not mind our grandiose building projects. I sincerely believe that none of our church buildings or cathedrals will ever surpass Solomon's magnificent Temple in terms of expense, beauty, and most of all significance. It is worth noting that Solomon built it with God's permission, provision, and guidance. The most important aspect of the Temple, however, was that the Ark of the Covenant - the symbol of God's presence, was behind the veil in the Most Holy Place.

None of us can forget the awesome glory that filled the Temple on the day of its Dedication, after the Ark of God was moved into its rightful place behind the veil amidst a glorious chorus of praise and worship. As magnificent as the outside and the furnishings of the temple were, there was no cloud of glory until the Ark was set in place, signifying to us that until we make room for God's presence to take pre-eminence in our lives and churches, nothing we do will receive His significant approval.

2 Chronicles 5:7 - 14

"The priests brought the ark of the covenant of the Lord to its place—to the inner sanctuary of the temple, into the Most Holy Place, under the wings of the cherubim ... and all the Levitical singers, ... all clothed in fine linen, with cymbals, harps, and lyres, stood to the east of the altar, and with them one hundred and twenty priests who were sounding with trumpets, it happened, when the trumpet players and singers made one sound to praise and give thanks to the Lord, and when they lifted up their voice with the trumpets and cymbals and all the instruments of music and praised the Lord saying, "For He is good and His mercy endures forever," that the house, the house of the Lord, was filled with a cloud. And the priests were not able to stand in order to serve because of the cloud, for the glory of the Lord had filled the house of God".

Since the Temple was in Jerusalem, and the Presence of God dwelled inside it, the city became the seat of both their religious and political governments. Three times a year, the whole nation convened at the Temple to worship, sacrifice and celebrate God's goodness over the nation. However, that same Temple became irrelevant and was ultimately torn down by Israel's enemies. This happened because the people chose to dishonor the presence of the Ark of God in their midst, by wantonly pursuing other gods and disregarding God's commandments. Once the glory departed, everything else lost its significance.

The good news, however, is that the glory of God will return once again to the Temple in Jerusalem, but this time it will manifest in the form of the Lord Jesus Christ at His second coming. In that day, the world's attention will once again be transfixed on that magnificent Temple in the city of Jerusalem, unlike it has ever been seen in history. Men and women alike, regardless of their title and status, including presidents and prime ministers, kings and queens, rich and poor will make a pilgrimage to that holy city to worship the One who sits on the throne in the Holy Temple.

As great as that day will be, God does not want us to wait until then before we experience His glorious presence. In fact, the greatest revelation we can have as believers is that God's ultimate goal for creating man was so that He could dwell in and manifest Himself through him. We have become the living, breathing temples of the living God carrying the "Ark" – His glorious presence with-in our *Holy of Holies*, which is our human spirit.

1 Corinthians 3:16 – 17:
"Do you not know that you are God's temple and that God's Spirit dwells in you? If anyone destroys God's temple, God will destroy him. For God's temple is holy, and you are that temple."

2 Corinthians 6:16:
"What agreement has the temple of God with idols? For we are the temple of the living God; as God said, "I will make my dwelling among them and walk among them, and I will be their God, and they shall be my people.""

Say this loudly after me, with faith and confidence:

"I am redeemed by the blood of the Lamb. I am the habitation and dwelling place of the Most-High God. My body is the tabernacle that hosts the presence and glory of the King of the universe. I AM A GLORY CARRIER!"

The Shekinah

Just like the Outer Court and Holy Place, there was a light that illumined the Most Holy Place. Unlike the former two, however, the light in the Most Holy Place was neither natural nor was it lit and tended by man. This light was supernatural, to say the least. It was the very glory of God, known simply as the *Shekinah*.

I sincerely believe this was the same light that manifested and guided God's people at various times throughout scripture. Moses encountered this light in the wilderness when God called him from the burning bush that was not consumed. This same light led the Israelites from Egypt as a pillar of cloud by the day, and as a pillar of fire by night. The Israelites also refused to approach this light out of fear when Mount Sinai burned with the consuming fire of God's presence. Furthermore, in the New Testament this same light rested on the 120 disciples in the upper room on the Day of Pentecost when the Holy Spirit invaded the earth with power and glory.

Acts 2:1 – 4:
"When the day of Pentecost arrived, they were all

*together in one place. And suddenly there came from heaven a sound like a mighty rushing wind, and it filled the entire house where they were sitting. And **divided tongues as of fire appeared to them and rested on each one of them**. And they were all filled with the Holy Spirit and began to speak in other tongues as the Spirit gave them utterance."*

It goes without saying that this Light, the **Shekinah**, was God Himself! In fact, we are told in the Book of Hebrews that *"our God is a consuming fire"* (**Hebrews 12:29**).

Every piece of furniture, including the Tabernacle itself, represented some aspect of the person and purpose of Jesus. This supernatural Light that brightened the Most Holy Place was indeed Jesus Himself. In fact, Jesus made this clear while He was physically on earth. He stated without equivocation that He was the Light of the world. When He returns to earth, He will do so as the very Light and Glory of God. We are told in the Book of Revelation that there won't be any need for the sun or moon to shine, because Jesus' physical presence will be all that is necessary to brighten the whole city. How glorious is that!

Revelation 21:22 – 23:
"And I saw no temple in the city, for its temple is the Lord God the Almighty and the Lamb. And the city has no need of sun or moon to shine on it, for the glory of God gives it light, and its lamp is the Lamb."

Isn't it amazing that not only is Jesus the Light of the world, but now you and I as born-again Spirit filled Christians, have also been called to become lights of the world? (**See Matthew 5: 14**). You and I are supposed to carry and manifest the **Shekinah** presence of God everywhere we go. It is time for the church to fulfill its end time prophetic mandate from Isaiah 60.

Isaiah 60:1 – 3:
*"Arise, shine, for **your light** has come, and the **glory of the LORD has risen upon you**. For behold, darkness shall cover the earth, and thick darkness the peoples; but the LORD will arise upon you, and **his glory will be seen upon you**. And nations shall come to your light, and kings to the brightness of your rising."*

It is time to arise from our apathy and complacency. It is high time to wake up from our laziness and sleepiness. It is time to begin once again to shine the light of God's manifested glory in a dark and perverse generation. You were born again to be the light of your world!

Ephesians 5:8 – 14:
"for at one time you were darkness, but now you are light in the Lord. Walk as children of light (for the fruit of light is found in all that is good and right and true) and try to discern what is pleasing to the Lord. Take no part in the unfruitful works of darkness, but instead expose them. For it is shameful even to speak of the things that they do in secret. But when anything is exposed by the light, it becomes visible, for anything

that becomes visible is light. Therefore, it says, **"Awake, O sleeper, and arise from the dead, and Christ will shine on you.""**

CHAPTER 13

BEYOND THE VEIL

As we advance further in our journey into intimacy from the Holy Place into the Most Holy Place, we encounter the veil that separates these two sections of the Tabernacle. As we highlighted in the introduction, the Tabernacle of Moses was actually divided into two main areas - the Outer Court and the Inner Court. The Inner Court was then divided into two parts - the Holy Place and the Most Holy Place, which was separated by a thick veil. Only the High Priest was allowed access beyond the veil once a year on the Day of Atonement.

The Spirit of God unveiled one of the most important revelations about the Tabernacle to me: The Father never intended to have a veil separating the Holy Place and the Most Holy Place. God's original desire and design was to make the Most Holy Place accessible to all His Priests.

We must constantly keep in mind that God has always considered His people as a nation, or kingdom of Priests. The only reason He chose to separate the tribe of Levi to become the sole custodians of the priestly mantle and function in the High Priestly office is because the entire nation of Israel refused to embrace this privilege and calling. This is important for us to understand because we are now called to be priests of the Most-High God. Unlike the nation of Israel, we must embrace this calling as a royal priesthood in order to have unlimited and unrestricted access to God's throne room in order to encounter His Presence. This awesome privilege has been made possible because Jesus paved the way by removing the veil through His blood.

1 Peter 2:5 – 9:
*"you also, as living stones, are being built up a spiritual house, a holy priesthood, to offer up spiritual sacrifices acceptable to God through Jesus Christ... But you are a chosen generation, **a royal priesthood**, a holy nation, His own special people, that you may proclaim the praises of Him who called you out of darkness into His marvelous light."*

Revelation 1:5 – 6:
*"...To Him who loved us and washed us from our sins in His own blood and has **made us kings and priests** to His God and Father, to Him be glory and dominion forever and ever. Amen"*

Hebrews 10:19 – 20:

*"Therefore, brethren, having boldness to enter the Holiest by the blood of Jesus, by a new and living way which He consecrated for us, **through the veil**, that is, His flesh."*

Let me reiterate that the veil in both the Tabernacle of Moses, and in Solomon's magnificent Temple, was never God's original desire and plan. Have you ever wondered why God said He would restore the Tabernacle of David, instead of the Tabernacle of Moses? God prophesied through the Prophet Amos that in the last days he would restore the Tabernacle of David. This prophecy was also affirmed by James, the brother of Jesus, in the Book of Acts.

Amos 9:11:

"On that day I will raise up the tabernacle of David, which has fallen down, and repair its damages; I will raise up its ruins and rebuild it as in the days of old."

Acts 15:16 – 17:

"After this I will return and will rebuild the tabernacle of David, which has fallen down; I will rebuild its ruins, and I will set it up; so that the rest of mankind may seek the Lord, even all the gentiles who are called by My name, says the LORD who does all these things."

This prophecy bothered me for quite some time because I assumed that if God was going to restore any tabernacle it would be that of Moses. After all, Moses was one of the most significant patriarchs in Israel's history, and the one originally tasked to build the

Tabernacle as it was revealed to him. So why would God rather choose to rebuild David's Tabernacle, and not Moses'?

I believe the main reason has to do with the one significant difference between the two tabernacles. Both tabernacles had several similarities. They both had an Outer and Inner Court. David's tabernacle, however, was unique in that it had no veil dividing what we might consider the Holy Place and the Most Holy Place, where the Ark of God resided. Unlike Moses' tabernacle, as we will soon discuss, the Ark of God was in plain sight within the tent King David had erected for it. After becoming king over all of Israel, David appointed Priests and Levites to minister unto the Lord in worship and prayer before the Ark with musical instruments non-stop, day and night.

1 Chronicles 16:1 – 4:
"And they brought in the ark of God and set it inside the tent that David had pitched for it, and they offered burnt offerings and peace offerings before God... Then he appointed some of the Levites as ministers before the ark of the Lord, to invoke, to thank, and to praise the Lord, the God of Israel."

This act of David so much pleased the heart of God that God vowed to establish His kingdom rule through David's descendants forever. This promise will be fully manifested when Jesus, who was a descendent of David, returns to establish His eternal kingdom on earth. God finally found someone who would not only replicate His throne on earth but would also make it the main focus and center of attraction of his life. David was not satisfied to worship God from afar. He refused to allow any veil to restrict his access to the presence of God. He, like Moses and a few others before him, chose to go beyond the veil to encounter the presence of God. I like the way Mike Bickle of the *International House of Prayer* puts it, "David's occupation was the king of Israel, but his pre-occupation was the presence of God"₄. David makes it clear concerning what was the most motivating factor in his life. His one desire was not to enjoy the perks of his position, but to experience the privilege of having unlimited and unrestricted access to the Ark of God. His desire was to be able to sit in God's presence without any veil of separation.

Psalms 27:4:
"One thing have I asked of the Lord, that will I seek after: that I may dwell in the house of the Lord all the days of my life to gaze upon the beauty of the Lord and to inquire in his temple."

The question we need to ask ourselves is - if the veil in Moses' Tabernacle was not God's original intention, then why did He instruct Moses to include it when he built the tabernacle? The answer to this pertinent question can be found in the book of Exodus.

We have already noted that Moses was instructed to build the tabernacle according to the pattern that he was shown on the mountain. I believe that just like John the Revelator, Moses was given a heavenly tour of God's throne. Based on what was revealed to John in the book of Revelation, we can all attest to the fact that there is no mention of a veil separating God's throne. In Revelation Chapter 4 we find both the twenty-four elders - who represent the redeemed bride of Christ, and the angels worshipping God and ministering before the throne. This is the vision King David had for his tabernacle and surely must have been what Moses also saw.

Since Moses did not see a veil, God must have included this detail after the children of Israel declined His invitation for a face-to-face encounter when they arrived at Mount Sinai. Instead of drawing near to God with hearts full of expectation and joy, they drew back in fear and asked Moses to be their go-between. They thus created a human *veil* between them and the fiery presence of God. Since they were not ready to embrace their priestly calling, God had no choice but to "hide" Himself from their sight by creating the veil in the tabernacle. As a result of this He gave Moses and Aaron - the first High Priest, exclusive access to His presence. This privilege was then extended to the lineage of High Priests who were only chosen from the Tribe of Levi.

It is amazing that God's wisdom to include the veil in the tabernacle was later confirmed after the tabernacle's construction.

Exodus 34:29 – 35:
When Moses came down from Mount Sinai... Moses did not know that the skin of his face shone because he had been talking with God. Aaron and all the people of Israel saw Moses, and behold, the skin of his face shone,

and they were afraid to come near him. But Moses called to them, and Aaron and all the leaders of the congregation returned to him, and Moses talked with them. Afterward all the people of Israel came near... And when Moses had finished speaking with them, he put a veil over his face. Whenever Moses went in before the Lord to speak with him, he would remove the veil, until he came out. And when he came out and told the people of Israel what he was commanded, the people of Israel would see the face of Moses, that the skin of Moses' face was shining. And Moses would put the veil over his face again, until he went in to speak with him.

As this scripture reveals, the children of Israel were unable to endure the glory of God that shone on Moses' face as a result of his encounter with God's presence on the mountain. The residue from the Shekinah Glory shone so bright on Moses' face that the children of Israel ran and hid themselves just as they had initially done after receiving God's corporate invitation to encounter Him at the mountain. The only way they could be close to Moses and communicate with him was if a ***veil*** was placed over his face. If God's chosen people - who he had called and separated unto himself, could not behold the glory of God upon an ordinary man's face, except while being covered by a veil, then how could they behold God's glory face to face without a veil separating them? For this reason, it was necessary for God to place a veil between the Holy Place and the Holy of Holies.

The good news is that through the sacrifice of Jesus Christ - our Passover Lamb and High Priest, we no longer need a veil to prevent us from a face-to-face encounter with God's glory. We now have unrestricted access to God's presence. In fact, I believe this is the main reason why Jesus came, to remove the veil of partition that separated us from the glory of God. One of the most important details during Jesus' crucifixion that stands out among many others is what happened in the Temple after He sighed and gave up the ghost.

Matthew 27:50 – 51:
*"Jesus, when he had cried again with a loud voice, yielded up the ghost. And, **behold, the veil of the temple was rent in twain from the top to the bottom**; and the earth did quake, and the rocks rent"*

The veil was torn violently into two so that God's original purpose, to unify the Holy Place and the Holy of Holies, would be fulfilled. No longer is the Shekinah the exclusive purview of the High Priest. Now it is also accessible to all of God's priests if they are willing to experience Him fully without any human intervention.

You and I were created to live in the glory of God. Like Adam and Eve, we were made to encounter God in all His fullness and majesty, to become partners in advancing His agenda on the earth. The Apostle Paul tells us exactly what we lost when sin invaded the consciousness of man. If we discover what we lost because of Adam's disobedience, then it is reasonable to assume that this is also what Jesus, our last Adam, came to restore.

Romans 3:23:

"For all have sinned, and come short of the glory of God."

What man lost, and what Jesus came to restore was the glory of God. Jesus restored the ability for humanity to freely fellowship with divinity once again but without a *veil* separating them. The very substance that held the relationship between God and man together, was the same substance that created man - - the glory of God. Adam was created in the glory and for the glory, and therefore could only function effectively when connected to the glory. If we do not recognize this as our highest purpose and begin to pursue it, then this leaves us with only a religious experience - void of true power and real substance.

God's goal is for us to experience Him like Moses did, without the veil. It is interesting that the bible says that when Moses was with the people, he would put the veil on, but when he went into the Tabernacle to commune with God face-to-face, he would remove it. If this Old Testament Patriarch could have this kind of access, then I believe you and I - who have been redeemed by the blood of Jesus, should have even greater access to partake in this awesome experience in the glory of God. This amazing experience is what God definitely expects us to have. This is the whole point of our redemption, to return to our Eden like identity so we can once again commune with God and become equipped to take dominion in the earth.

Psalms 8:3 – 6:

"When I look at your heavens, the work of your fingers, the moon and the stars, which you have set in place, what is man that you are mindful of him, and the son of man that you care for him? Yet you have made him a little lower than the heavenly beings and crowned him with glory and honor. You have given him dominion over the works of your hands; you have put all things under his feet."

One of the most revealing scriptures concerning God's will for you and I as it relates to us encountering the fullness of His glory was given by the Apostle Paul to the Corinthians. The Apostle Paul used the experience we just described of Moses encountering God's glory to allude to the fact that we as the redeemed children of God ought to also experience an even greater dimension of that glory.

2 Corinthians 3:5 – 18:

"Not that we are sufficient in ourselves to claim anything as coming from us, but our sufficiency is from God, who has made us sufficient to be ministers of a new covenant, not of the letter but of the Spirit. For the letter kills, but the Spirit gives life. Now if the ministry of death, carved in letters on stone, came with such glory that the Israelites could not gaze at Moses' face because of its glory, which was being brought to an end, will not the ministry of the Spirit have even more glory? For if there was glory in the ministry of condemnation, the ministry of righteousness must far exceed it in glory. Indeed, in this case, what once had

glory has come to have no glory at all, because of the glory that surpasses it. For if what was being brought to an end came with glory, much more will what is permanent have glory. Since we have such a hope, we are very bold, not like Moses, who would put a veil over his face so that the Israelites might not gaze at the outcome of what was being brought to an end. But their minds were hardened. For to this day, when they read the old covenant, that same veil remains unlifted, because only through Christ is it taken away. Yes, to this day whenever Moses is read a veil lies over their hearts. But when one turns to the Lord, the veil is removed. Now the Lord is the Spirit, and where the Spirit of the Lord is, there is freedom. And we all, with unveiled face, beholding the glory of the Lord, are being transformed into the same image from one degree of glory to another. For this comes from the Lord who is the Spirit."

My dear friend, this is our portion and destiny, to leave our Outer Court experience in order to draw closer and go deeper in our encounter with the Lord **beyond the veil**.

Ever since the Lord revealed this to me, I have pondered on several questions. When Jesus breathed His last breath and the veil was rent asunder, how many people in Jerusalem - on that fateful and awesome day, ventured into the Temple to behold the glory that was now open and available to all? How many people had the same heart and overwhelming desire of both Moses and David - to be close to the fiery presence of God? How many would risk everything just to get a glimpse of the light that had been hidden from their view for so many generations? If you were alive during that day, would you have approached that light, especially with the understanding you now have about God's original plan? If the answer is yes, then God's offer still stands today. You and I have a standing invitation from the King of Glory - to come boldly to his throne of grace **beyond the veil** both personally and corporately. We are encouraged to come without hesitation and reservation in order to behold and experience His light, love, and life. Through this experience we will become what we behold and will be better equipped to release the same glory to people every place we go.

CHAPTER 14

FATHERS

According to the Apostle John, the next stage of maturity for the believer in their journey of intimacy with God is **fatherhood**, which is experienced in the Holy of Holies.

1 John 2:12 – 14:
"I write unto you, little children, because your sins are forgiven you for his name's sake. I write unto you, fathers, because ye have known him that is from the beginning. I write unto you, young men, because ye have overcome the wicked one. I write unto you, little children, because ye have known the Father. I have written unto you, fathers, because ye have known him that is from the beginning. I have written unto you, young men, because ye are strong, and the word of God abideth in you, and ye have overcome the wicked one."

It is no coincidence that the trait associated with being a **father** is that *"you have known Him that is from the beginning"*. As we have already seen, the trait associated with children in the Outer Court relates to their sin and overriding need for forgiveness. In the Holy Place, however, the trait for young men relates to their strength to overcome the evil one. Finally, in the Holy of Holies we come face-to-face with the Father Himself.

It is in the Holy of Holies that we become one with the Father in our thoughts, attitudes, and actions. We do not only know **about** Him, but rather we get to know Him. This term **know** - when used in scripture, depicts a level of knowledge of a person or thing that goes beyond intellect or mental assent. It reveals a relationship that is based on experiential knowledge, and most often denotes a level of intimacy such as sexual intercourse, such as described in Genesis 4.

Genesis 4:1:
"And Adam knew Eve his wife; and she conceived, and bare Cain, and said, I have gotten a man from the Lord."

To **know** someone therefore means to have both an intimate and intricate relationship based on personal history and experience. What I know of, or about a person is not just based on what I have been told or read but based on my own personal history and experience with that person. When true intimacy occurs between two individuals, a confidential exchange takes place in which others are not privy. There is a level of honest dialogue to which others are not invited. Transparency is developed exclusively between the two, which creates an atmosphere of openness and trust. There are no secrets, everything is laid bare and the two become one. This may describe the kind of relationship that either exists, or should exist between married couples, but more importantly the kind of intimate relationship the Father yearns for with His people.

The Father wants to share His secrets with you and I as we share ours with Him. Knowing the God-Head - the Father, the Son, and the Holy Spirit, is God's ultimate desire for His people, and should therefore be our highest priority in life. This was Paul's most urgent desire and prayer which he expressed in Philippians 3:10 *"...that I may know Him..."*. What amazes me is that Paul made this declaration at the end of his ministry, rather than at the beginning. At the time of this statement, Paul had already been walking with and serving the Lord for over thirty years. He had witnessed every kind of miracle you could think or imagine. In fact, he already had his out of body experience where he was transported to the third heavens where he saw and heard things, he was not permitted to share with anyone (***See 2 Corinthians 12:1***).

After thirty years of earth-shaking ministry, the Apostle Paul declares *"I want to know Him"*! Didn't he already **know** Him? Of course, he did. Paul's statement, however, reveals that the more you know God, the more you recognize how little you know of Him. This realization becomes the impetus to a deeper quest to pursue an even greater knowledge of Him. He was not satisfied with a shallow revelation of the one who loved and called him into the ministry. Neither was he content to remain in the Outer Court or Holy Place experience. He wanted to go beyond the veil and into the Most Holy Place in order to encounter the very essence of God the Father.

I believe Paul's understanding of God's ultimate purpose for us to progressively grow in our knowledge of Him from childhood to fatherhood became the overriding theme in his many letters to the early church. For example, when he writes about the function and purpose of what we call the *"Five-fold Ministry Office Gifts"*. Paul makes it abundantly clear that the main purpose and function of those privileged to walk in the five-fold ministry office gifts is to **equip** or prepare the church to enter the state of **fatherhood**. This level of maturity is where the church - the Bride of Christ, is intimately acquainted with God through His Son Jesus.

Ephesians 4:11 – 13:
*"And he gave some, apostles; and some, prophets; and some, evangelists; and some, pastors and teachers; For the perfecting of the saints, for the work of the ministry, for the edifying of the body of Christ: Till we all come in the unity of the faith, and of the knowledge of the Son of God, unto a **perfect** [mature] man, unto the measure of the stature of the fullness of Christ: That we henceforth be no more children... may **grow up** into him in all things, which is the head, even Christ"*

It bears repeating that God's ultimate goal for His church is that we would cease to only experience Him as the Way in the Outer Court as **children**. God desires and intends for us to mature in our intimacy with Him by advancing past the Holy Place, until we are face-to-face and one with Him beyond the veil, in the Holy of Holies. God's hope and plan for you and I is that we become **fathers** who know, love, and serve Him not out of obligation, but simply because we have become one with him. If we follow God's plan, we will be able to see what He sees and feel what He feels. As a result of our love for Him, we will be compelled to say like Isaiah said, *"here I am Lord, send me"* (Isaiah 6:1).

CHAPTER 15

FRUIT OF THE SPIRIT
(MUCH FRUIT)

As we discussed in the Introduction, there are three levels of fruit that the Lord requires us to bear as we encounter Him in the three parts of the Tabernacle in our journey of intimacy with Him. As mentioned in John 15, the three levels of fruit are - fruit, more fruit, and much fruit.

We have already seen that in the Outer Court we bear the *fruit* of repentance or righteousness as we encounter Jesus as the Way and as Savior. In the Holy Place, we bear *more fruit* as we encounter Jesus as the Truth and the one who sanctifies us for priestly service. In the Holy of Holies, we bear *much fruit* - which is the fruit of the spirit. Before you enter this precious place called the Holy of Holies, you need to encounter Jesus - not just as the Way, or the Truth, but as the Life.

In Galatians 5, the Apostle Paul masterfully describes what the fruit of the spirit is, as opposed to the works, or fruit of the flesh.

Galatians 5:22 – 23: (ESV)
"But the fruit of the Spirit is love, joy, peace, patience, kindness, goodness, faithfulness, gentleness, self-control: against such things there is no law. And those who belong to Christ Jesus have crucified the flesh with its passions and desires".

Based on Paul's description, many in the church have tried to explain what the fruit of the spirit is. They have surmised that there are nine different *fruits* of the spirit, which are – *love, joy, peace, patience, kindness, goodness, faithfulness, gentleness, and self-control.* This cannot be the case, however, since Paul used the singular reference for fruit, and not the plural form. In other words, Paul must have been referring to a singular individual fruit as the expression of the life of one who is living according to the spirit, and not according to the flesh. Furthermore, he made a distinction between the works, or *fruits* of the flesh (plural) and the *fruit* of the spirit (singular).

If this is true, then why does he seem to highlight nine unique characteristics of the fruit of the spirit, in much the same way he enumerates at least eighteen attributes of the works of the flesh? By pointing out what the fruit of the spirit is, Paul also includes the individual components that make the fruit complete. Through the inspiration of the Holy Spirit according to Paul, the fruit of the spirit is LOVE! He then introduces us to the eight characteristics of love. In other words, love is the fruit that we bear as we consistently abide in the presence of God. The individual expressions of love are then manifested as joy, peace, longsuffering, gentleness, etc. These eight attributes must consistently be working in and through the believer's life in order for God's agape love to be fully expressed through their lives. Just like in the natural mangoes and bananas are fruits that are best enjoyed when they are fully ripe, so also the fruit of the spirit is fully matured in us when we allow all eight expressions of love to thoroughly operate and be manifested in our lives. Paul confirms this when he explains what love is in his initial letter to the Corinthian church.

I Corinthians 13:4 – 8:

"Love suffers long and is kind; love does not envy; love does not parade itself, is not puffed up; does not behave rudely, does not seek its own, is not provoked, thinks no evil; does not rejoice in iniquity, but rejoices in the truth; bears all things, believes all things, hopes all things, endures all things. Love never fails..."

Another interesting anecdote worth mentioning is that most of our bible translations state that *"the fruit of the Spirit is love..."*. I believe it should rather be stated as *"the fruit of the spirit is love..."*. You may be wondering what the difference is. The first statement suggests that the fruit is produced by the Holy Spirit, whereas the latter suggests the fruit is produced by YOU - through your regenerated human spirit.

Remember that man is a three-part being, namely spirit, soul, and body. As the great Pentecostal pioneer Howard Carter perfectly described, *"man is a spirit; he possesses a soul, and he lives in a body"*5. When you and I receive Jesus as Lord and Savior, it is our spirit that becomes regenerated and born again, through the infusion of the Holy Spirit. The Holy Spirit currently resides or dwells in our spirit. In fact, the bible makes it clear that our human spirit and the Holy Spirit become fused together or become one at the point of our conversion and salvation.

1 Corinthians 6:17:
"But he who is joined to the Lord is one spirit with Him."

At this point of conversion, there might not be any initial or visible changes in your soul, or body. You still may have most, if not all, of your worldly or sinful attitudes, mindsets, and proclivities; and your physical appearance will definitely look the same. However, as you begin your journey of maturity into intimacy with the Lord, you move from the Outer Court of your salvation experience into the Holy Place experience of sanctification.

This is where your soul - your mind, will, and emotions, is sanctified and purged from its worldly tendencies by the Spirit of Truth - which is represented by the Menorah, and the word of God - which is represented by the Table of Showbread. This process of sanctification continues as you consciously and deliberately seek for more of God's presence and influence in your life through intimacy. Once you begin to be led by the Holy Spirit, living by your natural senses becomes less and less appealing. On the other hand, living by your regenerated human spirit, becomes more and more exciting and exhilarating.

This is the distinction Paul was alluding to when differentiating between the works of the flesh and the fruit of the spirit. He was simply distinguishing between the evidence of the life of one who lives according to their flesh - which is dictated by our degenerate, corrupt human senses, compared to the life of one who lives according to their regenerated human spirit – which is dictated by the Holy Spirit. This life is infused with the light, love, and life of God's Holy Spirit. The fruit of that life, therefore, is love - which expresses itself in joy, peace, longsuffering, patience, gentleness, goodness, faithfulness, meekness (humility), and temperance (self-control).

This should not be a surprise since the bible states that, "God is love". If God is love and we are created in His image and likeness, then we have been created in the image of Love. Furthermore, if we have been born of God, as the John declares in 1 John, then we have been born of Love.

If we will allow our human spirit to fellowship daily in God's presence, then we will also become love personified.

1 John 4:4 – 17:

"Beloved, let us love one another, for love is of God; and everyone who loves is born of God and knows God. He who does not love does not know God, for God is love... No one has seen God at any time. If we love one another, God abides in us, and His love has been perfected in us. By this we know that we abide in Him, and He in us, because He has given us of His Spirit...And we have known and believed the love that God has for us. God is love, and he who abides in love abides in God, and God in him. Love has been perfected among us in this: that we may have boldness in the day of judgment; because as He is, so are we in this world."

Once you are in the Holy of Holies, the flesh is crucified, and the spirit is allowed to take full control of your life. This is the result of several things, mainly because the flesh cannot endure the very presence and glory of God. Secondly, since God is a Spirit, only your spirit can have unrestrained access to God. Your human spirit, according to Proverbs 20:27, is the "candle of the Lord". It is this **candle** that truly has fellowship with the Shekinah glory of God. In the Holy of Holies, it takes light to fellowship with Light, as spirit encounters Spirit.

It is amazing what the presence of the glory of God will do to whatever is exposed to it for any period of time. It will produce life in any dead thing, and will even cause the driest wood to bud, bloom, blossom, and produce fruit. This is what happened to the rod of Aaron, the first High Priest of Israel.

As the children of Israel were still wandering in the wilderness on the way to their Promised Land, some of the leaders began to murmur and complain against God's chosen leadership of Moses and Aaron. As they continued to undermine and rebel against them, God finally had enough and decided to settle the issue once and for all. His instruction to Moses was to ask all the elders of the various tribes - including the Levites, God's chosen priestly tribe, to submit their rods to be placed overnight inside the Ark of God within the Tabernacle of Moses. These dry, dead rods represented the symbol of their authority. Whichever elder's rod budded and blossomed in the presence of the GLORY overnight and bore fruit, was therefore God's undisputed and approved leader. When the congregation of Israel woke up the next day, low and behold they discovered that only Aaron's rod had budded and blossomed, while the others' remained as dry and dead as before.

Numbers 17:1 – 8:

"And the Lord spake unto Moses, saying, speak unto the children of Israel, and take of every one of them a rod according to the house of their fathers, of all their princes according to the house of their fathers twelve rods: write thou every man's name upon his rod. And thou shalt write Aaron's name upon the rod of Levi: for one rod shall be for the head of the house of their fathers. And thou shalt lay them up in the tabernacle of the congregation before the testimony, where I will meet with you. And it shall come to pass, that the man's rod, whom I shall choose, shall blossom and I will make to cease from me the murmurings of the children of

Israel, whereby they murmur against you...And it came to pass, that on the morrow Moses went into the tabernacle of witness; and, behold, the rod of Aaron for the house of Levi was budded, and brought forth buds, and bloomed blossoms, and yielded almonds"

What does this tell us as God's chosen and ordained priests today? When we stay in God's glorious presence long enough, we will also begin to bud, bloom, blossom, and become fruitful. When you encounter the Life-giving force of God's presence, everything dead in you receives new life and what is dry becomes fruitful, especially your spiritual life.

When you are intimately acquainted and connected to the Life of God, you will not struggle to produce fruit, especially the **much fruit** of love. In other words, as Jesus explained in His discourse with His disciples in John 15, fruitfulness becomes second nature and is the by-product of your connection to the Source of Life.

Oh, that this would become our experience as God's people! Refuse to stay in the Outer Court, or even the Holy Place in your experience with the Lord. Press into the Holy of Holies where there is real Life and much fruit. You will not struggle to love God and man. Neither will you struggle to love friend or foe.

Psalm 92:13, 14:
"Those that be planted in the house of the Lord shall flourish in the courts of our God. They shall still bring forth fruit in old age; they shall be fat and flourishing."

CHAPTER 16

PRESENCE-BASED
PRAYER
(KNOCKING)

We previously discussed the kinds of prayers that represent the Outer Court and Holy Place. In the Outer Court – **petition-based prayer**, or asking, is the predominant focus of the newborn believer. As he or she progresses in their journey of intimacy with the Father, **power-based praying**, or seeking, should become their focus in the Holy Place. Once they proceed however, beyond the veil into their Holy of Holies experience with the Lord, they suddenly become more preoccupied with the Person and Presence of the Lord. This is the final level of prayer Jesus described as **knocking** in Matthew 7:7.

In **person-based praying**, the focus is primarily on God's face and not His hands. In other words, the praying person is more interested in getting to know God's personality and discovering His attributes, opposed to ascertaining what God can or will do for them. Once engaged in this type of prayer, the believer is captivated by the beauty of God's Holiness, and just wants to hang around the Throne Room to experience the magnificence of His glory. This my friend is what the patriarchs like Moses, David, and Paul experienced with great joy and delight. They came face-to-face with God's glory, beauty, and majesty; nothing else could even compare to this wonderful encounter.

We also briefly talked about Moses and his life changing request of the LORD to show him His glory. Through his prayer encounters, Moses had experienced enough of God's power to know that having His presence without the Promised Land was far more valuable than riches. This was the impetus of his request to God when the Lord became fed up with the children of Israel and declared He would no longer accompany them to the Promised Land. In essence the Lord was going to withdraw His Shekinah Glory which had guided them up until this point as a Pillar of Fire by night, and as a Cloud by day. The Lord's response deeply disturbed Moses, which led him to request an audience with the Lord. Although Moses' request has been a popular refrain among Pentecostal Christians over the decades, there has been, however, very little understanding or appreciation of what Moses was actually asking of the Lord.

Exodus 33:13 – 18:

*"Now therefore, I pray, if I have found grace in Your sight, show me now Your way, that I may know You and that I may find grace in Your sight. And consider that this nation is Your people." And He said, "My Presence will go with you, and I will give you rest." Then he said to Him, "If Your Presence does not go with us, do not bring us up from here. For how then will it be known that Your people and I have found grace in Your sight, except You go with us? So we shall be separate, Your people and I, from all the people who are upon the face of the earth." So the Lord said to Moses, "I will also do this thing that you have spoken; for you have found grace in My sight, and I know you by name" And he said, "**Please, show me Your glory**."*

In order to fully appreciate Moses' dialogue with the LORD, we will need to pay close attention to the specific words of his request. Let us look closely at his words. At first, Moses asked the Lord to reveal His ways, not His acts, so that Moses might know Him. Secondly, he asked for God's presence to go with him, without which he refused to move an inch. Although the masses probably would not have minded settling for God's promises without His presence; Moses, however, chose to stay in the dangerous wilderness with God's presence rather than to pursue the Promised Land without it. Finally, Moses asked the greatest thing of all that the Lord would show him His glory.

Many, including myself, have prayed and sang songs asking, ***show us thy glory, oh Lord***. Based on my own experience, however, I believe when well-meaning Christians pray or sing this to the Lord, they are actually asking the Lord to demonstrate His miraculous power again as seen throughout the scriptures or heard about through the testimonies from the saints of old. This is far from Moses' original intent.

At this point in Moses' career, he had experienced the miraculous power of God to not only lead the children of Israel out of Egyptian captivity, but to also sustain them in the wilderness. Moses had witnessed the hand of God upon his life in many signs and wonders. Just to name a few among many, Moses saw - ten plagues cripple the greatest nation at the time; the Red Sea divide in half for over three million people to cross over on dry ground; manna rain down from heaven to feed millions of men, women, and children; and water gush out of a rock to quench the children of Israel's thirst. Although all these signs were encouraging, they still were not enough to satisfy Moses' desire for God. He wanted more. More than anything Moses desperately wanted to know the Person behind the power more intimately.

Prayer is a two-way communication - we speak to God, AND then we wait and listen for Him speak back to us. God enjoys having a dialogue with us much more than hearing our many monologues. After you have spoken to God in prayer, are you willing to linger a little while longer in His presence in order to hear what He will say to you? Trust me, you will learn to enjoy prayer more if you truly believed there was someone on the other end of the line who not only desires to talk back to you, but who loves you unconditionally, and also enjoys being with you. Like young Samuel, we need to cry out, "speak Lord, your servant is listening".

Many years ago, I was greatly impacted by a message Suzette Hattingh shared concerning intimacy in intercession. Suzette used to be a part of the late world-renowned evangelist Reinhard Bonkke's Christ For the Nations Evangelistic Ministries. She would lead teams of intercessors to pray for his evangelistic campaigns, especially in Africa. She would train and lead hundreds, if not thousands, of indigenous 'Prayer Warriors' before, during, and after the crusades that saw millions come to Christ, thousands healed and delivered from demonic oppression, and even the dead raised back to life. Her intercessory spirit really inspired me as a young up and coming intercessor. In this particular message, she shared an experience she had that really revolutionized my understanding of intercession and confirmed my own desire for greater intimacy with God beyond any ministry pursuits.

One day after praying and interceding for almost six hours on behalf of many nations, Suzette got up from the floor and headed for the door. As soon as she laid her hands on the doorknob, she heard the unmistakably still small voice of the Lord saying to her, *"Suzette, how about me?"*. She was startled at this question and quizzically responded to the Lord, *"Lord, I've been in this room with you praying and interceding for almost six hours. What do you mean by 'what about me'?"* The Lord responded again saying, *"I know you have been in here praying for many things and I have heard and answered you. BUT what about me?"* Suddenly the light bulb came on in her heart as she understood exactly what the Lord was saying. You see just like many of us, she had mastered the art of praying/interceding and receiving answers from the Lord. However, what she had not learned yet was that there was another level of prayer in which the Lord takes much more delight. She knew how to move His hands, but had she learned how to move His heart? What the Lord was communicating to Suzette that day was that after accomplishing her intercessory duties, He wanted her to stay awhile just to fellowship and enjoy His presence. The Lord still had somethings He wanted to share with her heart-to-heart, like a father with his daughter or a husband with his wife just hanging out with no specific agenda.

Nonetheless, according to Suzette, this experience marked a turning point in her life and ministry. I must say it also marked me once I heard her tell it. No longer will ministry pursuits take the place of intimacy with my Father. In fact, Suzette went on to share how due to this radical shift in her approach to intercession, she never endured another burn-out in ministry. How can one burn out when their gaze is transfixed on the One whose eyes burn like fire?

During this formative time of my walk with the Lord, I would visit a church in my city where their doors were opened during the day for prayer. I was amazed at how many people came in to pray feverishly and passionately but then would immediately walk out when they were finished. I thought to myself, why don't they linger a little while longer in silence to minister to the Lord and wait to receive from Him? Now I do understand that time constraints and busy schedules often do not allow us to just wait a while in His presence after we pray. I also appreciate the fact that the Lord can speak to us even while we are on the move, so I'm not in any way criticizing anyone. I was, however, left with the impression that if most of these people would tune their ears right, they would also hear the Lord asking them - like he did Suzette Hatingh, *"Alfred, what about me, or Angie, what about me?"*. Let me encourage all of us. There is another level we can get to in prayer, where words are not really needed - just a heart yearning to hear the voice of the One whom our soul loves.

CHAPTER 17

WORSHIP

We already discussed the kind of attitude of gratitude we should have as we journey throughout the tabernacle. Beginning in the Outer Court, the appropriate attitude we take on is thanksgiving. As we proceed through the Holy Place we enter in with an attitude of praise. As we approach the Most Holy Place – which is the apex of our intimacy experience with the Lord - the only attitude we can possibly have is worship.

In the architecture of the tabernacle, God instructed Moses to place a *Table of Incense* at the entrance of the Most Holy Place where the Ark of God was situated. The *Table of Incense* represented the aroma of worship from the people as they approached

God's throne. With the exception of the veil, the tabernacle on earth was a direct replica of the throne room in heaven. Therefore, the incense in the earthly tabernacle can also be seen in the heavenly temple, which represents the worship and prayers of the saints.

Revelation 8:1 – 4:

"When the Lamb opened the seventh seal, there was silence in heaven for about half an hour. Then I saw the seven angels who stand before God, and seven trumpets were given to them. And another angel came and stood at the altar with a golden censer, and he was given much incense to offer with the prayers of all the saints on the golden altar before the throne, and the smoke of the incense, with the prayers of the saints, rose before God from the hand of the angel. Then the angel took the censer and filled it with fire from the altar and threw it on the earth, and there were peals of thunder, rumblings, flashes of lightning, and an earthquake."

Why is worship not only the last, but highest and most important attitude we can have in our journey of intimacy? Worship is our greatest expression of love and devotion to the God who created us in His own image, and who sacrificed Himself to redeem us from our sin.

Although our human intimacy experience can never fully relate to any divine concept, allow me to describe the essence of worship. Worship is expressed as an overwhelming feeling of admiration for who God is, and extends far beyond what He has done, and will ever do for us.

As it relates to intimacy, if thanksgiving and praise represents the act of foreplay, then worship is the ultimate consummation of that relationship between God and man. The truth is, we were created to live in this state of worship. Adam and Eve had daily encounters with God in the Garden of Eden that totally consumed them with God's glorious presence. It is unfortunate that Adam and Eve were deceived by the enemy and distracted to shift their attention from their source to a false substitute. As a result of yielding to the enemy's deception and distraction, thus leading to their disobedience, Adam and Eve not only lost their spiritual awareness, but ultimately their intimacy with God. Even though they sought to rediscover it through their own human effort, which resulted in the birth of religion, Adam and his descendants have been unsuccessful in reuniting with the God who created them in His own image.

Man was created to worship God! Since the fall of mankind and his disconnect from God, men and women of all generations and cultures have tried to fill the emptiness they feel deep down on the inside of them. Religion especially, which is simply man's effort to find God, has sought to fill that void and failed. Materialism, humanism, and worldliness have also all failed to give man the same divine experience and ultimate satisfaction he once had in the Garden of Eden when he was one with God. The intimacy Adam had with His creator was gloriously pure and pleasurable. Humanity was in harmony with Divinity. There was no veil in between them. No secrets, no barriers, and no fears. Only LOVE!

Through this union, man was also empowered to live in accordance with the plan and purpose of His Creator. The void man continues to have today can therefore only be filled when he reconnects to the One who created him for His purpose and pleasure. And this, my friend, is why Jesus came.

Many are still searching for divine fulfillment by looking in all the wrong places. As much as man missed this original calling and purpose, God missed it even more. Therefore, God had to send His only begotten Son in human flesh to come and restore man's divine connection back to Himself. Above all else, the Father seeks us to worship Him. To help us in this effort, He instituted rituals for us to reconnect with Him through worship. All the religious rituals in the Old Testament were just a type and shadow of the real thing, which Jesus restored unto us. This is why His discourse with the woman at the well in John chapter 4 is one of the most important statements He ever made. He essentially abolished the system of worship that existed at the time, in order to introduce us to the Father's heart towards true worship.

John 4:19 – 26:

The woman said to him, "Sir, I perceive that you are a prophet. Our fathers worshiped on this mountain, but you say that in Jerusalem is the place where people ought to worship." Jesus said to her, "Woman, believe me, the hour is coming when neither on this mountain nor in Jerusalem will you worship the Father You worship what you do not know; we worship what we know, for salvation is from the Jews. But the hour is coming, and is now here, when the true worshipers will worship the Father in spirit and truth, for the Father is seeking such people to worship him. God is spirit, and those who worship him must worship in spirit and truth." The woman said to him, "I know that Messiah is coming (he who is called Christ). When he comes, he will tell us all things." Jesus said to her, "I who speak to you am he."

We usher in the manifest presence of God into our midst - both individually and corporately, when we worship the Lord with psalms, hymns, and spiritual songs. However, in its highest form, worship is a lifestyle of sincere obedience to the One whom we love with all our heart, soul, and might – the one true and living God. In other words, we seek to please Him in all we think, say, and do. Our highest form of worship therefore is expressed in our diligence in seeking to fulfill His will and purpose for our lives.

Your Alabaster Box

As mentioned at the beginning of the chapter, the *Table of Incense* was strategically placed at the doorway leading into the Holy of Holies. It is at this place of divine entry where God desires to release incense or a fragrance that would fill our entire atmosphere. When we worship, we release a sweet aroma that fills the Throne Room of God. This is the true essence of our worship. We see this perfectly illustrated in John's vision of the Throne Room in Heaven.

Revelation 4:8 – 9:

"And when he had taken the scroll, the four living creatures and the twenty-four elders fell down before the Lamb, each holding a harp, and golden bowls full of incense, which are the prayers of the saints. And they sang a new song, saying..."

Revelation 8:1 – 5:

"When the Lamb opened the seventh seal, there was silence in heaven for about half an hour. Then I saw the seven angels who stand before God, and seven trumpets were given to them. And another angel came and stood at the altar with a golden censer, and he was given much incense to offer with the prayers of all the saints on the golden altar before the throne, and the smoke of the incense, with the prayers of the saints, rose before God from the hand of the angel. Then the angel took the censer and filled it with fire from the altar and threw it on the earth, and there were peals of thunder, rumblings, flashes of lightning, and an earthquake."

As these scriptures aptly describe, the incense released in heaven represents the sincere worship and faith-filled prayers of God's redeemed people. When our worship is mixed with our prayers, it is amazing to see the effect they have not just in heaven, but also here on earth. The bible says there is a release of fire, thundering, and lightning that brings devastation to the kingdom of darkness. Do not take your worship and prayers lightly!

One of the most vivid pictures of worship in the bible was illustrated by the "sinful" woman who broke an alabaster box of perfume in the presence of Jesus and other religious leaders.

Luke 7:36 – 38:

"One of the Pharisees asked him to eat with him, and he went into the Pharisee's house and reclined at table. And behold, a woman of the city, who was a sinner, when she learned that he was reclining at table in the Pharisee's house, brought an alabaster flask of ointment, and standing behind him at his feet, weeping, she began to wet his feet with her tears and wiped them with the hair of her head and kissed his feet and anointed them with the ointment."

There are a few things we can glean from this woman's intimate expression of worship. First and foremost, she came boldly to where Jesus was, regardless of who else was there and what they thought of her. She came without hesitation or reservation. She was ready and willing to pour her heart and love upon the One who had rescued her from her sins. When we approach the throne room of God in worship, we must do so with boldness and confidence; and without caring what anyone else might think about us. Our audience is an audience of One. God is the object and sole focus of our worship because He alone is worthy.

Secondly, she wept at the feet of Jesus and wiped His feet with her hair. This represents the fact that in worship we are captivated by the awesomeness, beauty, and splendor of God. It is okay to be expressive and feel emotion in worship, as long as it's done for the benefit of the One we are worshipping, and not just for show to be seen by spectators. We should freely express our affections and gratitude to the Lord without any hindrances or restrictions.

Furthermore, according to **1 Corinthians 11:15**, a woman's hair is her glory. Therefore, by wiping His feet with her hair, she was surrendering her glory for His. Remember that Jesus' feet would have been quite filthy and even stinking by now after traveling a long distance. According to the traditional custom of the time, when guests entered a home after traveling a great distance the host of the home would wash each guest's feet. Jesus and the disciple's prestigious host had failed to wash their feet after they entered his home. This woman, however, was willing to stoop down and wash Jesus' feet with her tears and wipe them with her hair. In essence, she humbled herself and submitted her self-esteem to Him. When we approach God in worship, we should also be ready to cast aside our self-esteem, our status in society, as well as our degrees and pedigrees. We should come in humble submission to the King of Glory who has made us who we are and given us all we have. We need to follow the example of the twenty-four Elders in the Book of Revelation who continually cast their crowns at the feet of the Lord in worship.

Revelation 4:9 – 11:
"And whenever the living creatures give glory and honor and thanks to him who is seated on the throne, who lives forever and ever, the twenty-four elders fall down before him who is seated on the throne and worship him who

lives forever and ever. **They cast their crowns before the throne**, *saying, "Worthy are you, our Lord and God, to receive glory and honor and power for you created all things, and by your will they existed and were created.""*

Finally, and most importantly, she broke her expensive alabaster box of ointment and filled the room with the aroma of her sweet perfume. This alabaster box was her life savings from her unsavory profession. It represented her past, present, and future. When she broke it, she was saying to Jesus, *"take me as I am, and make me as you are. I am letting go of all that is on the inside of me, and I am giving it completely all to you. I am vulnerable and transparent right here in your presence, and I release all my secrets to you. All I am and hope to be is yours, I totally surrender myself - you can have it all".*

Worship, dear friend, is the greatest form of our intimacy with God. In true worship, there are no secrets. We allow the alabaster box of our flesh to be broken before the Lord and we lay our hearts bare before Him. God does not really care about what we say or do not say. He does not mind how loud or how soft we sing our worship songs. What He is after is the real attitude of our heart. The Lord desires the posture of our heart to be that of a sincere lovesick child who is ready to expose what is in their hearts to Him. The real you is what Jesus is after in worship. The real you is your human spirit - which God created in His image and likeness.

When you surrender yourself in worship, you release a sweet aroma like incense into God's nostrils.

We need to always remember that the worship the Father seeks, is worship that is done in *"spirit and truth"*. Let us break our alabaster box in His presence and allow our sweet-smelling worship to not only fill our earthly atmosphere during our personal and corporate times of worship, but more importantly, the very throne room of God in heaven. This kind of worship is what releases the tangible presence of God to impact regions and transform lives.

2 Corinthians 4:7:
"But we have this treasure in jars of clay, to show that the surpassing power belongs to God and not to us"

2 Corinthians 2:14 – 16:
"But thanks be to God, who in Christ always leads us in triumphal procession, and through us spreads the fragrance of the knowledge of him everywhere. For we are the aroma of Christ to God among those who are being saved and among those who are perishing, to one a fragrance from death to death, to the other a fragrance from life to life. Who is sufficient for these things?"

The Father beckons you and I to come beyond the veil to express our extravagant, heart-felt, and unrestrained worship. This is the place where we totally surrender to the Holy Spirit. It is the place where we experience superior joy and unlimited satisfaction. It is the place the Lord longs for you and me to find and ultimately settle. It is that secret place of intimacy with the Father. Are you ready to go Beyond the Veil with me? God richly bless you!

EPILOGUE

I hope you are ready to experience intimacy with God like never before. His arms are wide open to receive you and I in the most passionate love affair of all time. He is our bridegroom, and we are His spotless bride. Do not allow anything to stop you from experiencing this divine encounter. This is what God intended when He created you. This is why Jesus left His heavenly throne to come down and redeem you.

Three Postures of Intimacy

Before our dialogue is finished, I would like to offer you three ways in which we can position ourselves for intimacy with God. Not too long ago, the Lord revealed to me three different postures of intimacy displayed by Moses, Apostle John, and Mary the sister of Martha and Lazarus. These three biblical characters exhibited such an attitude of personal intimacy that, if imitated by you and me, will transform us like it did them.

1. Intimacy by His Side:

In this posture, we position ourselves by God's side. Moses exemplified this when He asked to see God's glory in **Exodus Chapter 33**. God's response to his audacious request was revealing.

Exodus 33:20 – 23:
*"But," he said, "you cannot see my face, for man shall not see me and live." And the Lord said, "**Behold, there is a place by me** where you shall stand on the rock, and while my glory passes by I will put you in a cleft of the rock, and I will cover you with my hand until I have passed by. Then I will take away my hand, and you shall see my back, but my face shall not be seen."*

Moses, unlike the rest of the Israelites, wanted a greater revelation and intimate knowledge of God. He wanted a face-to-face encounter with Him. The Lord, however, said this was not possible. Instead, there was a **place by His side** where Moses would be positioned to have a clear view of God's backside once all His glory passed by.

This posture of intimacy allowed Moses to see and do things with God that no other man in his generation was able to do. It allowed Moses to transcend from not only knowing the **acts** of God, but also the **ways** of God. This ultimately helped Moses develop an understanding of how God thinks and works.

Psalms 103:7:
"He made known his ways to Moses, his acts to the people of Israel."

When we position ourselves in *intimacy by His side*, it represents our partnership with God so that He can fulfill His agenda on earth. We are able to understand God's ways because we become one with Him. We grow in our identity as His sons and as His bride, and we become joint heirs. As a result, we are given a corresponding authority that allows us to operate as partners and co-laborers with Christ, and to exercise our kingdom dominion on the earth.

2. Intimacy at His Feet:

In this posture, we position ourselves at His feet. Mary exemplified this when Jesus visited her family's home in Bethany. While Martha was busy and encumbered with chores to prepare for the Master's visit, Mary instead assumed a posture of submission and experienced *intimacy at His feet*. While Martha chose to complain about her sister's unwillingness to help, Mary instead chose to sit at his feet and listen intently to His words. Jesus rebuked Martha, but commended Mary for focusing on what was more important – the Word of God.

Luke 10:38 – 42:

*"... Jesus entered a village. And a woman named Martha welcomed him into her house. And she had a sister called Mary, **who sat at the Lord's feet and listened to his teaching**. But Martha was distracted with much serving. And she went up to him and said, "Lord, do you not care that my sister has left me to serve alone? Tell her then to help me." But the Lord answered her, "Martha, Martha, you are anxious and troubled about many things, but **one thing is necessary**. Mary has chosen the good portion, which will not be taken away from her.""*

When we position ourselves at His feet, it represents our submission and surrender to His Word. We understand and grow in our identity as love slaves. In other words, we understand that even though we are His sons, we are also His servants. We are not just servants, but rather sons who serve. It is very important for us to understand and know the difference. If not, we will be prone to make the same mistake Martha made by confusing our busy church activities with spending quality intimate time in His presence. Although Jesus rebuked Martha, He was not saying that what she did was not important or appreciated. He simply wanted her to know that spending quality time in both the word and His presence is by far more important and necessary for true intimacy. By taking on this attitude of submission in His presence, it will help make us more effective servants. My dear friend, it is a true statement that *"lovers make better servants, and lovers will always out-work workers"*6.

This remarkable concept is highlighted in the Lord's assessment of the Church at Ephesus in the Book of Revelation. Although Jesus commended this church for their hard work and labor, He also reprimanded them for leaving their first love.

Revelation 2:1 – 5:
"To the angel of the church in Ephesus write: The words of him who holds the seven stars in his right hand, who walks among the seven golden lampstands. 'I know your works, your toil and your patient endurance... But I have this against you, that you have abandoned the love you had at first. Remember therefore from

where you have fallen; repent, and do the works you did at first..."'

Like Mary, the Church at Ephesus began in a place of **intimacy at His feet**, but somehow ended up overburdened with church activities like Martha. Over time they focused more on being busy doing the work of the Lord, instead of intimately fellowshipping with the Lord of the work.

If you find yourself in this position and have become too busy with the cares of life, more than spending quality time with the Lord, I encourage you to stop right now and repent to the Lord. Ask Him to remove the heart of Martha from you and give you the heart of Mary. Begin to intentionally make time to sit at His feet through prayer and His Word. I assure you that you will see a mighty transformation take place in your life. You may be a minister of the gospel who is busy doing the work of the Lord, but you know you have lost your first love. That love and passion you used to have when you could spend hours in His presence worshipping, praying, and studying the Word, has been replaced by mundane church activities and personal ministry pursuits. You are doing the work of the Lord alright, but you no longer sit and take time to fellowship with the Lord of the work. If that is you, the Lord gives you the same admonition He gave to the Church at Ephesus, ***repent and do the works you did before***. Above anything else, let us all yearn for the grace to be lovers of God first and foremost. Let us consciously endeavor to raise a generation of Marys and not Marthas. Come let us return to our first love!

3. Intimacy on His Chest:

In this final posture of intimacy, we position ourselves on His bosom, or chest. John the beloved Apostle demonstrated this posture of intimacy with the Lord when He laid his head on Jesus' chest during the Lord's last supper. This is significant because Jesus was at His lowest point in His thirty-three and a half years on earth. He was about to face the cruelest punishment any innocent or guilty human had ever endured. During this last meal and close fellowship with His disciples, Jesus knew he would soon be denied, betrayed, and ultimately abandoned in just a few hours. In the middle of the Last Supper, John laid his head on Jesus' chest as if to say, *"everything is going to be alright. I am here for you if you need me"*.

John 13:21 – 23 (AMPC):

"After Jesus had said these things, He was troubled (disturbed, agitated) in spirit and said, I assure you, most solemnly I tell you, one of you will deliver Me up [one of you will be false to Me and betray Me]! The disciples kept looking at one another, puzzled as to whom He could mean. One of His disciples, whom Jesus loved [whom He esteemed and delighted in], **was reclining [next to Him] on Jesus' bosom."**

When we position ourselves in **intimacy on His bosom**, it represents our ability to connect with God's heart, in order to feel His heartbeat for a lost and dying world. We are able to understand our oneness with Him, and also grow in our identity as His friends. In the Book of Proverbs, we are assured in knowing that *"...there is* *a friend who sticks closer than a brother"*, and that *"...a friend loves at all times"* **(Proverbs 18:24 & Proverbs 17:17).**

It is heartwarming to note that out of all the disciples who abandoned Jesus in His greatest time of need - including Peter who denied Him three times, only John remained by the Master's side throughout His ordeal leading up to the cross. All of them had voiced their loyalty to the end. Yet it was only John, with this one act of intimacy, who proved his loyalty and commitment to the end. It is no wonder that Jesus could entrust to John the care of His most valuable earthly relationship - His mother Mary.

John 20:26 – 27:
"When Jesus saw his mother and the disciple whom he loved standing nearby, he said to his mother, "Woman, behold, your son!" Then he said to the disciple, "Behold, your mother!" And from that hour the disciple took her to his own home"

When reading the Gospel of John, it has always intrigued me that the writer often referred to himself as *"the disciple whom Jesus loved"*. This was so important to him that John wanted his identity to be associated with the knowledge of the Master's love for him. I believe He was confident of this fact because He knew how much He loved Jesus. He understood that there was no way He could out love God, who is the personification of love. Whatever love he had for the Master, came out of the overflow of God's love for him. After having the privilege of reclining on Jesus' bosom and experiencing ***intimacy on His Chest***, over sixty years later John was able to pen in his epistle that *"We love Him because He first loved us"* **(1 John 4:19)**.

My dear friend, let the revelation of the love of God captivate you even now as you read this book. Like John, may the knowledge of His love empower you to love Him to the point of laying your head on His bosom and in order to feel His heartbeat for lost humanity. May you see yourself as His friend and close confidante. May you be someone the Lord can trust with His most valuable and precious goods in the whole world - the souls of men, women, and children who do not know him, and are destined for hell. May our love and oneness with Him compel us with an eternal endeavor to place the jewel of a soul in the crown of our Lord Jesus Christ. Let us draw closer to His bosom and experience a greater level of intimacy. Jesus desperately wants to share His passion with us.

Isn't it interesting to know that out of all the characters we mentioned - including Abraham, each was referred to as friends of God in the bible? God is looking for some intimate friends He can share His secrets with and entrust His kingdom mandates. The Lord is patiently waiting for you and me to enter into intimate fellowship with Him, not just anywhere, but BEYOND THE VEIL!

Epilogue

APPENDIX
THE TABERNACLE OF MOSES

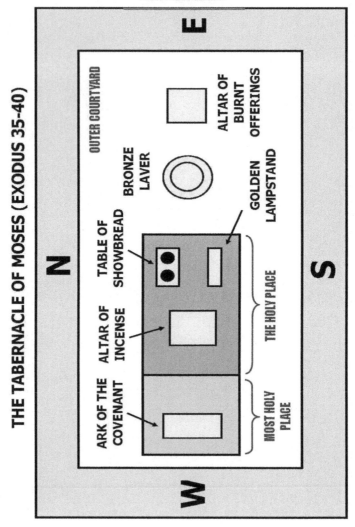

THE TABERNACLE OF MOSES (EXODUS 35-40)

ENTRANCE GATE

E

N

S

W

OUTER COURTYARD

ALTAR OF BURNT OFFERINGS

BRONZE LAVER

GOLDEN LAMPSTAND

TABLE OF SHOWBREAD

THE HOLY PLACE

ALTAR OF INCENSE

ARK OF THE COVENANT

MOST HOLY PLACE

THE TABERNACLE OF DAVID

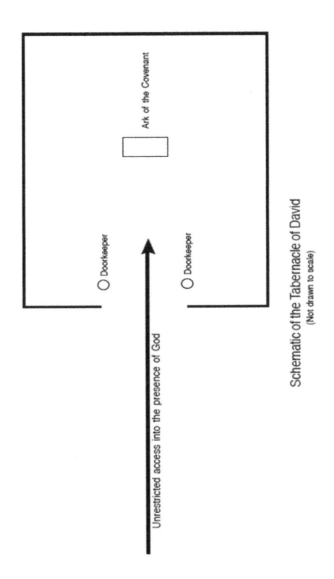

Schematic of the Tabernacle of David
(Not drawn to scale)

NOTES

OTHER BOOKS BY THE AUTHOR

In this wonderful book on prayer, Alfred Tagoe explores the 7 types of prayers contained in the "Lord's Prayer" which will connect you to the Person, Presence, and Power of God. This journey of discovery will transform your prayer life from one of mundane repetitiveness to one of absolute joy in the presence of God.

"The Blessed Life is more than just a book about the Sermon on the Mount, it's a book taking you into the heart of God's desire to prepare for Himself a people who rightly exemplify Him and the great rewards they'll encounter as each beatitude fashions them into a pure and spotless Bride made ready for Her soon and coming King" – Louis Kayatin

All titles above can be purchased on Amazon or on our church website, www.oasisoflovecc.org

Made in the USA
Columbia, SC
01 May 2021